"In this vital and beautiful workbook, Erika Shershun guides us through the process of understanding our sexual trauma, and ultimately working toward a place of thriving. What really emerges for me from these exercises is that she is equipping survivors with the tools and processes that embolden us to move beyond surviving to flourishing. Erika is inviting survivors on a powerful journey of transformation—and I'm grateful to her for entrusting survivors to be the drivers of that process."

—**JoEllen Chernow**, cofounder and codirector of Survivors Know

"Erika Shershun has written a much-needed, empowering resource for sexual assault survivors. Her *Healing Sexual Trauma Workbook* explains how trauma impacts the body, mind, and soul. It provides a comprehensive array of worksheets, body-based exercises, and support tools for recovery. It addresses concerns common to survivors that are often overlooked in treatment. And it compassionately offers the guidance, hope, and support that all survivors of sexual assault need and deserve."

—**Susanne Babbel, PhD, MFT**, author of *Heal the Body, Heal the Mind;*
and blogger for www.psychologytoday.com

"Erika Shershun has managed to create an invaluable handbook for the many courageous survivors of sexual trauma who are working hard to find their way back to a life of normalcy. What is particularly notable about this, among so many others, is that Shershun knows the territory directly, having found a way to access her own considerable gifts of healing both herself and others. She provides a clear path toward finding one's way."

—**Don Hanlon Johnson, PhD**, professor of somatics in the School of Consciousness and
Transformation at the California Institute of Integral Studies (CIIS); and author and
editor of several books, including *Bone, Breath, and Gesture* and *Body, Spirit, and Democracy*

"This workbook is a must for anyone struggling with unhealed trauma. Erika gives tangible tips to safely move through trauma in an empowering and validating way. Learning to listen to your body and emotions is scary and hard, but Erika's workbook makes this practice gentle, which is so needed. So many trauma survivors will be able to reclaim a part of themselves after finishing this."

—**Stevie Croisant**, founder of We Are HER

"I highly recommend this compassionate and gentle book to both clients and practitioners as a tool for healing sexual abuse using somatic practices. This step-by-step guide is an excellent source of information to help survivors better understand their body's reactions. In addition, it offers valuable instructions on everything from grounding to tapping exercises, and from practicing self-compassion to how to handle triggers and flashbacks."

—**Beverly Engel**, licensed therapist, and author of *Escaping Emotional Abuse* and *It Wasn't Your Fault*

healing
sexual trauma
workbook

SOMATIC SKILLS TO HELP YOU

FEEL SAFE IN YOUR BODY,

CREATE BOUNDARIES &

LIVE WITH RESILIENCE

ERIKA SHERSHUN, MFT

New Harbinger Publications, Inc.

Publisher's Note

This publication is designed to provide accurate and authoritative information in regard to the subject matter covered. It is sold with the understanding that the publisher is not engaged in rendering psychological, financial, legal, or other professional services. If expert assistance or counseling is needed, the services of a competent professional should be sought.

NEW HARBINGER PUBLICATIONS is a registered trademark of New Harbinger Publications, Inc.

New Harbinger Publications is an employee-owned company.

Copyright © 2021 by Erika Shershun
New Harbinger Publications, Inc.
5720 Shattuck Avenue
Oakland, CA 94609
www.newharbinger.com

Cover design by Amy Shoup; Illustrations by Calvin Lai;
Acquired by Jess O'Brien; Edited by Gretel Hakanson

Library of Congress Cataloging-in-Publication Data

Names: Shershun, Erika, author.
Title: Healing sexual trauma workbook : somatic skills to help you feel safe in your body, create boundaries, and live with resilience / Erika Shershun.
Description: Oakland, CA : New Harbinger Publications, [2021] | Includes bibliographical references.
Identifiers: LCCN 2020057925 | ISBN 9781684036509 (trade paperback)
Subjects: LCSH: Sexual abuse victims--Rehabilitation. | Sexual abuse victims--Psychology. | Psychic trauma--Treatment.
Classification: LCC RC560.S44 S544 2021 | DDC 616.85/83690651--dc23
LC record available at https://lccn.loc.gov/2020057925

Printed in the United States of America

26   25   24

10   9   8   7   6

Dedicated to you, along with the many survivors

I've had the honor to work with and learn from.

Contents

Introduction

It takes courage and perseverance to heal from sexual assault. It is that very courage and perseverance that's led you to this book. My long struggle to heal from sexual trauma drew me to a career as a licensed marriage and family therapist who specializes in working somatically with survivors. The word "somatic" means relating to the body, and somatic therapy draws on feelings, thoughts, and bodily sensations. I've written this book because it breaks my heart to see survivors struggling, as I did, to find the necessary tools to heal. I've compiled the practices I've found most effective in my work to share with you so you too don't lose precious time searching.

Many of the exercises in this book ask you to bring attention to your body and what sensations are present. You might be wondering, *Why my body when my thoughts originate in my brain?* given the brain is commonly regarded as the center of thought. We work with the body and its sensations, as well as feelings and thoughts, because your brain is interconnected with your entire body through the peripheral nervous system and signals from your body's physiological processes. Your brain isn't an isolated organ in your head; it's interconnected with your heart-brain, your gut-brain, and your nervous system, all interwoven with the physiology and movements of your entire body (Siegel 2012).

I know firsthand that talk therapy alone will not alleviate all the symptoms of trauma. It's necessary to address what's happening in your body as you're making meaning not only with thoughts but also with bodily sensations; one influences the other. Since your experiences are interwoven with one aspect influencing another, together affecting the whole, you can't simply think or will away the intrusive symptoms of trauma. The whole system must be included in healing. The body-mind is where transformation takes place.

Author and bodyworker Deane Juhan (2003) summed up this interconnectedness beautifully, "The skin is no more separated from the brain than the surface of a lake is separate from its depths; the two are different locations in a continuous medium.... The brain is a single functional unit, from cortex to fingertips to toes. To touch the surface is to stir the depths" (43).

Healing from sexual assault is a journey that takes time. There will be twists and turns along the way. You may have a breakthrough, followed by a time of reprieve; then a new discovery, detail, or memory will surface. This can feel devastating, like a big setback, and when your nervous system is in a depressed state, you may lose hope of ever healing from sexual trauma. But the journey's not linear; it's not about crossing a finish line. Each time you encounter what feels like a setback, another piece of the trauma is stepping into the light of day to be healed. It's your preceding success, however small, that allowed for this new challenge to be faced. It's like peeling off layers of an artichoke, eventually you'll come to the most wonderful center, the undefended heart.

I'm grateful to the #MeToo movement for shining a light on this long-hidden underbelly of humanity. Illuminating this dark truth has helped many find the courage to give voice to the unspeakable, and ultimately seek support to heal. Although we have a long way to go, we've traveled so far from when I was first assaulted. Back then, we had never heard the terms "acquaintance rape" or "date rape"; internalized shame kept us in isolation believing self-defeating thoughts like, *This is proof of my unworthiness,* or *I must be to blame.* There was no chorus of others' voices to help normalize our traumas. I cringe as I write the word "normalize"; there's nothing normal about these violations, yet the frequency with which they occur leaves a wake of violated and traumatized souls in their paths— souls that need to know they're not alone, that their symptoms are not evidence of a sickness within, but rather a sign of a disease throughout our culture. You are not alone.

How to Use This Book

As you progress through the exercises in the book, listen to and honor what your body's telling you. If you start to feel overwhelmed, give yourself permission to stop and use the exercises that calm your nervous system. Remember, you're always the one in charge. You have choice.

It's best to go through the book in sequence as the practices build on one another. It's okay to skip ahead if there's an area you're anxious to get to, such as triggers or working with a particular emotion, and then pick back up where you left off.

There are practices I ask you to do daily, and some are as needed. If you put the time and effort into the practices, you'll progress more rapidly and have better results. You're always practicing something. You may as well be intentional about it.

Many of the practices and worksheets are available for download at the website for this book, http://newharbinger.com/46509. There, you'll also find lots of bonus practices to further integrate healing into your life.

Finally, it's okay if you don't, but if you have a friend or therapist to share your process with, I strongly encourage you to include them. You may feel vulnerable at times, but their support will help you heal.

CHAPTER 1

Learning to Feel Safe in Your Skin

Embarking on this journey of healing is an act of courage and bravery. It's possible you don't feel like it's courageous. It may feel as though you have no choice or as if it's an act of desperation. Perhaps you're struggling at work to maintain focus due to intrusive thoughts and flashbacks. Perhaps friends or family are keeping their distance because they don't know what to say or how to help or because you've been acting differently and they don't know why. Your unpredictable emotions may be making you feel out of control and wanting to isolate. Perhaps your partner's feeling rejected because you've lost interest in intimacy, and it's just too painful and triggering for you. These are just some of the ways symptoms can show up.

What's telling you that you want to heal?

_____

_____

_____

_____

_____

Healing from Sexual Assault

By choosing to work toward healing, you're choosing to reclaim a wounded part of yourself that's suffered deep violation and betrayal. Healing won't always come easy or feel good, but if you stick with it, the rewards will be great. You might gain a sense of being safely embodied; of feeling like yourself again; of recovering your focus and concentration; of reclaiming your sexuality; of feeling the freedom to be creative, playful, and spontaneous; or of feeling connected to others, to nature, and to life.

What are your goals for healing or growth? Take a moment to reflect then jot them down.

_____

_____

_____

_____

_____

As you progress toward these goals, remember this journey truly is a courageous act of resilience, defiance, and strength.

I'm a sexual assault survivor who struggled for years to find the tools needed to heal, all the while being impacted by the trauma in subtle and sometimes not so subtle ways as it shaped my relationships and life. I spent my twenties moving from place to place, traveling at every opportunity, at times even putting myself in danger, until I realized I'd been desperately trying to escape my past and myself. I thought, as so many survivors do, *There must be something wrong with me.* I scraped the money together and started seeing a series of therapists over a period of seventeen years, during which time I was diagnosed with depression. Other than a brief mention of the sexual assaults as part of history-taking, the sexual traumas were not processed and remained for the most part locked away from my conscious awareness, all the while impacting my life choices. Finally, the trauma refused to be ignored, and I experienced a series of bodily symptoms including fainting, dissociation, flashbacks, and vertigo. While attending grad school, the flashbacks increased, activating shortness of breath with painful constriction in my throat, trembling and tears, or other intense emotions all within seconds, leaving me feeling humiliated and often judged. This is when I began gaining access to and accumulating on my own the tools I needed to heal.

You might not recognize the symptoms I described because the effects of trauma differ from person to person. I suspect you have a good idea of what trauma feels like for you. Still, you may not understand what causes your symptoms or how to heal from them. My goal is to help you recognize patterns of sensations, feelings, and thoughts that arise when you begin to get activated or overwhelmed and to provide you with the tools and information needed to aid in your healing.

I invite you to pause for a moment, place your hands on your heart or give yourself a hug, take a deep yet gentle breath, and gift yourself a little validation, recognition, and praise for beginning this process. Stay with this feeling a little longer as you take it in. Notice if you're having a hard time absorbing it. If so, try to let a small bit in, even just 1 percent.

What Trauma Is

Trauma is the result of overwhelm to your system. It's not cognitive; it's biological. It's about fear and your ability to cope. There's no time to think when facing a threat; your primary responses are instinctual. Peter Levine, PhD, author of the pioneering book *Waking the Tiger,* has spent over forty years studying stress and trauma and is responsible for many discoveries in the field. Levine observed that an animal in the wild will instinctually shake after escaping a life-threatening event to discharge accumulated energy and then go on its way as if nothing happened. He realized that like other mammals, when faced with an overwhelming event, the human body must complete a primitive process: preparing for the event, reacting to it, and then discharging the accumulated energy once the threat has passed (Levine 1997). Trauma results when this process is thwarted in some way, such as not being able to react or discharge the accumulated energy after the threat has passed.

When you're overwhelmed by an experience, without the capacity to fully release sensations and emotions that accompany the traumatic event, the undigested experience is stored on a cellular level. Instead of discharging the energies of the overwhelming experience through your body, you might tense up, inhibit, or repress. You may feel under threat even when you're not in danger as the incident gets triggered by bodily sensations that are experienced in the present and activate emotional states. In this way, the experience of trauma is not about the past. It's about a body that continues to behave and organize itself as if the experience is happening in the moment.

Do you ever feel under threat even when you're not in danger? If so, describe a time when this has happened to you.

_____

_____

_____

_____

When trauma is beyond one's capacity to cope, especially when the trauma's perceived to be or is life threatening, post-traumatic stress disorder (PTSD) can emerge. Approximately 50 percent of sexual assault survivors develop PTSD. I believe the numbers are higher given the research does not take into account those who develop it years after the initial trauma. Having symptoms appear years after the assault(s) can in some ways be even more disorienting. Whether it appears within a month or years later, PTSD is equally disrupting and devastating. The good news is that healing is possible, and it's never too late to begin the process.

Even if you didn't consciously feel your life was in danger, most survivors were systematically groomed to comply or complied out of fear. If you were molested, you might not have felt your life was being threatened, yet you may have been dependent on the abuser for your survival. If you're an acquaintance-rape survivor, you might not have felt as though your life was in imminent danger, yet you may have frozen in terror from the shock of the betrayal. This freeze is a survival response that often leads to PTSD, and both instances feel life threatening to your nervous system.

There are many factors that contribute to how resilient you are and whether PTSD will develop after trauma, including the ability and opportunity to have taken some kind of action during the traumatic event without putting yourself at further risk of danger. Genetic inheritance (character strengths and traits), intergenerational trauma (trauma passed down in your DNA from your more recent ancestors), developmental trauma (C-PTSD), complex trauma (prolonged repeated experiences of interpersonal traumas), and oppression (sociocultural, institutional, and/or economic exclusion or marginalization) all contribute to how resilient you are. You can see that each item is largely beyond your control. In other words, it's in no way your fault if you're suffering from symptoms of trauma or PTSD. You're not now and never were to blame because you didn't have a choice. Thankfully you now have choice in what actions you take to heal.

Take a few slow deep breaths and know there's no shame in suffering from trauma or a diagnosis of PTSD. It doesn't have to be a life sentence. With the proper treatment, symptoms can improve or heal altogether. If you suspect PTSD or are experiencing unmanageable symptoms, it's important you seek additional support (if possible) from a trained psychotherapist, psychologist, or psychiatrist. Since psychological issues are inseparable from what's occurring in your body, the exercises in this book can be an important aspect of your overall treatment. If you're in counseling, I recommend discussing this workbook with your therapist.

Understanding Your Trauma Symptoms

Let's take a look at some of the symptoms of trauma. Think of the early symptoms as your body's way of trying to get your attention. It's letting you know something's off and it's time to get help or support. If you've effectively suppressed the overwhelming event, symptoms may take years to appear. Some can show up soon after the trauma; others may take much longer to develop. These symptoms don't always indicate trauma and aren't meant for diagnostic purposes, yet if they persist, it may be a sign. I've divided the symptoms into five categories. Circle any symptoms you've experienced since the traumatic event(s).

1. Hyperarousal

- heightened startle response

- frequently scanning the environment or watching for trauma reminders

- feeling on edge or having feelings of anxiety

- related physical symptoms, such as a racing heart, upset stomach, or headaches

- becoming irritable, quick to anger, or aggressive

- difficulty concentrating

- difficulty sleeping

- risky or impulsive behaviors

2. Reexperiencing the trauma

- distressing thoughts and feelings about the trauma

- emotional distress after being triggered by a reminder of the trauma

- physical responses after being triggered

- flashbacks

- nightmares

3. Avoidance of trauma reminders

- avoidance of people, places, or things related to the trauma

- avoidance of activities related to the trauma

- avoidance of conversations related to the trauma

- suppressing thoughts related to the trauma

- using drugs, alcohol, or food to suppress uncomfortable thoughts and emotions

4. Negative thoughts or feelings

- excessive blame toward oneself or others related to the trauma

- loss of memory related to the trauma

- loss of interest in activities

- difficulty experiencing positive feelings

- feeling isolation or disconnection from surroundings

- excessive negative thoughts about oneself

- excessive negative thoughts about the world

5. Mental and physical health issues
(These symptoms usually take longer to develop and were likely preceded by some of the earlier symptoms.)

- immune system problems

- some endocrine problems, such as thyroid malfunction and environmental sensitivities

- asthma

- skin disorders

- digestive problems, such as IBS, acid reflux, and SIBO (leaky gut)

- chronic pain, chronic fatigue, or fibromyalgia

Take a nice deep breath, feel the support of the chair you're sitting in or the ground your feet are on, and then take your time as you look over the symptoms you've identified.

Do you have a lot of symptoms in one category, some in several categories, or symptoms in each? Write down the categories with the most symptoms you've identified.

_____

_____

Are there any symptoms you want to add?

_____

_____

How do you feel about having these symptoms?

_____

_____

_____

How would your life be different if you didn't have these symptoms?

_____

_____

_____

As you review this list, know that you're not alone in your symptoms. Although you may not know their names, there are many others traveling this path along with you. The symptoms differ for each person, but all are common among survivors. I've seen many people overcome the symptoms in the first four categories, with symptom reduction or restored health in the fifth.

Trauma, like stress, creates an excess of adrenaline in the body that, if untreated, can lead to adrenal exhaustion, depression, and thoughts of suicide. Symptoms can be off and on, triggered by stress, or they can be constant. *If you have thoughts of suicide please seek help immediately. You can call the National Suicide Prevention Lifeline at 1-800-273-8255.*

Trauma is showing you where the wounds are and where to place your attention and care. Since symptoms can continue on and new ones may appear years after the overwhelming event, trauma has been referred to as the gift that keeps on giving. That is until you're resourced enough to be aware that it's time and you're ready and able to do the work needed to heal. I suspect that's what drew you to this book. Next I'll help you explore how you identify when you're safe.

How Do You Know If You're Safe?

We become a victim when choice has been taken away from us. If you were molested or assaulted, your very survival was threatened. You did not see or could not find a physical or psychological way out, a way to safety. If you could have escaped the situation and prevented the abuse, you would have. You're not to blame because you couldn't prevent what happened to you. The reality is if you're a survivor, you were threatened, manipulated, coerced, or forced into sexual abuse, even if the perpetrator was someone who claimed to love you. Now, as you consciously begin the process of healing, you're claiming or reclaiming empowered choice.

After suffering this devastating violation and betrayal, feeling safe is understandably challenging. If you experienced childhood sexual abuse, you may have lost or never fully developed a sense of safety. If you're an adult survivor, you may no longer have access to a felt sense of safety. As a result, it's possible and even likely for you to be safe but feel as though you're not safe. Conversely, if you don't know the cues and the feeling of "not safe" is familiar, it's possible to be in an unsafe situation but feel as though you're safe.

In spite of the shattering betrayal, you need to develop or reconnect with a sense of safety to move into your healing. Without a sense of safety, you can get stuck in survival mode unable to access the fullness of who you are, your creative expression, your ability to take on new challenges and to grow, and your sense of connection to others and all of life.

We will explore the following questions in greater detail as you move forward in the book. For now, take a few minutes and begin to notice all of the ways you determine if you're safe.

What tells you that you feel safe? Do you feel calm, present, engaged, or social, or are there other signs?

_____

_____

_____

What tells you that you don't feel safe: your thoughts, emotions, senses, intuition, or bodily responses?

_____

_____

_____

What thoughts are you aware of when you don't feel safe?

_____

_____

_____

What thoughts are you aware of when you feel safe?

_____

_____

_____

What happens in your body when you don't feel safe? Does your breath get shallow or your heartbeat speed up or slow down? Do you want to run away or lash out, or do you feel like you can't move? Does your stomach, heart, or throat feel tight or uncomfortable? These are just a few of many possibilities.

_____

_____

_____

What happens in your body when you do feel safe? What does it feel like when you're calm?

_____

_____

_____

To feel safe internally is to feel safe in your skin, to be safely embodied. When you're safe externally and feel safe within, you can relax and be present to whomever or whatever you wish to focus your attention on. You move along a continuum from survival to creativity.

Assessing Safety in Your Relationships

Assaults often happen within the context of a friendship, first date, or first relationship. The 2010 National Intimate Partner Sexual Violence Survey found that 51 percent of female-identified victims reported being raped by an intimate partner and more than 40 percent reported an acquaintance. That means more than 91 percent of rapes were committed by someone the victim knew. Slightly more of the male victims reported being raped by an acquaintance (52 percent) or a stranger (15 percent). Most rapes happen when victims are young, impressionable, and vulnerable, with more than 79 percent of female victims being first raped before the age of twenty-five, and more than 42 percent of those happening before the age of eighteen (Black et al. 2011). It doesn't help that around the time of puberty, young girls are culturally conditioned to be agreeable. This conditioning does not encourage empowered boundary-making, choice, and agency, all vital in keeping yourself safe.

Your past conditioning, your experiences, and any current trauma may unwittingly lead you into relationships that repeat abusive patterns. For this reason, it's important to watch out for red flags. One way is to observe how your partner reacts when you change your mind or say no. If their response goes beyond disappointment into a sense of ownership or entitlement or they act controlling, it's likely a red flag, one that can lead to increasingly abusive behavior.

If you're in a relationship where safety is questionable, it will be very hard to make progress in your healing. To assess whether your safety's at risk, go to http://newharbinger.com/46509 to download and complete the "Assessing Safety in Your Relationships" worksheet. If you want immediate support or need to seek nonemergency help, you can call RAINN's national sexual assault twenty-four-hour hotline at 1-800-656-4673. Their trained volunteers will listen to your concerns and may be able to help you determine the best course of action.

Connecting to a Sense of Safety

In a perfect or better world, it would be your birthright to feel safe within your skin when no danger is present. Unfortunately, the trauma of sexual assault, or more precisely the perpetrator(s), has robbed survivors of this basic freedom. If you're a survivor, it can be incredibly challenging to know when you're safe and when you are not. Building a foundation of safety within yourself is among the most important resources to cultivate in healing from incest, sexual assault, and other forms of trauma. Feeling safe within your body allows you to be present to do the work needed to free yourself from the challenging and disruptive symptoms of trauma and PTSD.

Many survivors automatically numb, cut off, or dissociate (split off, disconnect, or separate) from their bodily experience. They may have collapsed, immobilized, or frozen during the trauma. If this happened to you, it may help to know this was your nervous system doing its job to ensure your survival. Once the trauma ended, feeling any sensations associated with the assault may be too overwhelming. You may continue to numb, cut off, or dissociate much of the time in a subconscious effort to ease or escape the pain. Or you may constantly be on high alert (hypervigilance), scanning your surroundings and tracking the facial expressions and movements of anyone you come into contact with for signs of danger. In either case, you seldom have access to any sense of safety and pleasure.

The cost of hypervigilance, numbing, and dissociating is losing access to your body's wisdom, the subtle yet informative messages your body offers by way of sensations and emotions. Another cost is relational. You may have a hard time making or maintaining connections with and trusting others, or you may cling to others in unhealthy codependency. When you lose access to your emotions and sensations, you also lose access to self-agency—you're no longer empowered. This is why it's so important that you begin with restoring a sense of physical safety.

Take time now to reflect on which of the responses I described (hypervigilance, numbing, dissociating) feel most familiar to you. Or perhaps you have one to add.

_____

_____

_____

There's a rich healing journey ahead of you. For now, it's only necessary you start to understand the importance of coming into safety and residing in your body. Even if you've never felt safe before, I want to help you begin to cultivate a feeling of safety from within. Let's begin by breaking down the steps of the practice "Coming into Safety," which is the foundational practice for feeling safe and a practice that I'll refer to often in this book.

Grounding

Grounding is the feeling of being physically and energetically connected to Earth. Your body is both matter and energy, and even though gravity is always pulling you downward toward Earth's surface, you may have lost or never developed a strong energetic connection. When you experience an intense trauma, such as incest or sexual assault, your energy is pulled upward, resulting in a loss of connection to Earth's welcoming support just when you need it most. Any sense of safety and trust may have been replaced with a feeling that the ground's been pulled out from underneath you, that you're unable to support yourself. You may feel off balance or that you've been knocked off your feet (perhaps literally). You may or may not be aware of these feelings, yet your body may organize in relation to them. Take a moment now to notice if you can connect with a sense of grounding.

- If seated, feel your weight on the surface you're sitting on and notice how this surface is supporting you.

- Drop your awareness down and feel your feet on the ground.

- Try moving your weight from side to side, from back to front, and around in a circle. Notice where you feel most centered and supported and what tells you this.

- Sense the pull of gravity and your connection with the ground below. If you can't sense it, try imagining it.

- Now imagine that the Earth is friendly and welcoming you as it supports you, that it's telling you you're at home. How does this feel?

- Take some time to reflect on your experience of grounding.

_____

_____

_____

_____

A loss of grounding isn't unique to survivors. Our culture reveres the brain, so generally our energy is focused higher in the body. When most of your energy is centered upward in your head, an imbalance in the autonomic nervous system is created, producing anxiety and an overreactive sympathetic nervous system. The sympathetic nervous system is what initiates the fight-flight response, which can cause you to feel out of control or overly impacted by your emotions as your heart rate increases and your prefrontal cortex, which controls executive functioning, goes offline. This upward shift of energy is heightened by trauma and can become chronic, eventually leading to depression or a slew of other symptoms. Grounding helps bring awareness back into your body, increasing nervous system regulation and supporting reconnection on all levels of experience.

Do you ever feel easily distracted, scattered, spacey, or excessively focused on the needs of others, or experience thoughts that get stuck on repeating the same themes? These can all be signs that too much of your energy is pulled upward. An ongoing grounding practice will help regulate the flow of energy in your body, which in turn helps eliminate energy blockages that can lead to illness. Over time grounding will improve your ability to access and feel your emotions, while at the same time bringing a greater sense of safety as you experience what's present in a more embodied way.

Although not usually the case when healing from sexual trauma, it's possible to be overgrounded, where your energy is not flowing upward from Earth's magnetic field. Symptoms of overgrounding include a sense of heaviness, along with feelings of being stuck, trapped, or hopeless. Energy is being pushed downward as though the Earth is a place to hide. These same feelings can be present if you feel undergrounded; however, they won't include the weightiness. In both cases what's needed is to begin to grow a sense of the Earth as welcoming, nourishing, and supportive.

Unlike your thoughts, your body exists 100 percent of the time in the present. Grounding helps you come into your body where you can be fully present. It's from this grounded foundation that you'll begin to cultivate embodied safety, a solid base of grounded support from the Earth and within, allowing for forward momentum in your healing. This allows you to feel the breadth and depth of your connection to yourself and others as you draw strength and guidance from your body and the living Earth. Here is a simple method for grounding that I encourage you to explore.

PRACTICE: **Toe Tapping**

Toe tapping is a practice to strengthen grounding and originated in traditional Chinese medicine (TCM) and qigong.

- Lie down on a flat surface, facing up. Scan your body and take note of what you're feeling, without judgment.

- Allow your hips and legs to rest easily, hips loose and feet a few inches apart.

- Rotate your feet inward and tap the sides of your big toes together before letting your legs and feet roll back out. Your toes should meet just below the nail at the widest part of your big toe.

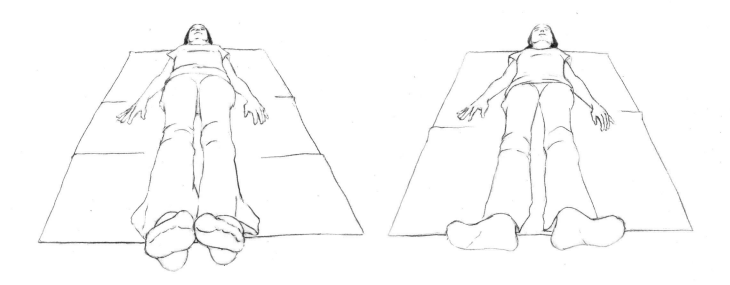

- Be sure to rotate your feet and legs in and out from your hips (not just your ankles). This helps loosen the hips, which supports grounding.

- While you find your rhythm, it can help to pick up the pace as you continue to tap your big toes together. The momentum will make it easier to sustain.

- If you wish, close your eyes and relax as you continue tapping. You might try listening to fast, rhythmic music while tapping to the beat. When you have the hang of it, you can do breathwork, combine mindfulness practice, read, or watch a show as you tap if you prefer.

- Continue tapping for a minimum of five minutes. Ten minutes is excellent, yet five is beneficial and far better than not at all.

When you've stopped tapping, scan your body again and notice if you feel any subtle or significant shift in your energy level. For instance, you may have felt tired when you started and are now energetic enough to accomplish a task, you may be winding down for the day and notice you feel more relaxed, or you may observe a subtle tingly feeling of movement somewhere in your body.

What do you notice?

_____

_____

Toe tapping is meant to be an ongoing daily practice. You can tap once, twice, or several times a day. The results can seem subtle, but don't let that fool you. This practice is more powerful than you might realize. The effects are cumulative, taking up to a year to experience the full benefits. When change is gradual, we often fail to realize the impact of a practice, yet if we think back to where we were a year ago in relation to grounding, anxiety, and the fight-flight response, we will see the progress. Experiencing the gradual results of this practice was the first thing that made me hopeful when I was at the lowest point in my recovery.

Orienting

When you orient, you focus your attention on an object, sound, or person, consciously or unconsciously turning toward the source. Throughout your day, you make choices, not always consciously, about what you orient toward and what recedes into the background. For instance, you may orient toward a smile or toward a frown, toward potential signs of danger or avoiding the signs, or toward receiving a compliment or dwelling on a criticism.

If you have experienced intense sexual trauma, you've likely developed habituated orienting responses resulting from some of the ways you learned to cope, for example focusing in a hypervigilant manner on the subtlest of shifts in facial expressions in an attempt to assess whether you're safe, hearing and recounting only negative and critical comments from your partner while missing any positive cues, or losing focus at work due to compulsively orienting toward a coworker's movements behind you because that was the direction of the assault. Although these orienting habits helped you survive during and following the trauma, your circumstances have likely changed, and these patterns may no longer serve you.

The more you repeat a pattern, the more habituated it becomes. There's an often-quoted phrase from neuropsychologist Donald Hebb that sums this up, "Neurons that fire together wire together." So, if for instance, you habitually orient toward fear, you will grow more neural pathways in your brain that reinforce your pattern of looking for signs of fear in others, your relationships, and your environment. On the other hand, if you cultivate a practice that brings you into a state of calm, you'll grow more neural pathways that reinforce your ability to orient toward signs of calm in your relationships, your environment, and yourself.

Orienting toward reminders of past trauma can bring about distress, fear, and discontent. If you consciously direct your attention to where you want it to go, you'll begin to break habitual patterns of moving toward signs of interpersonal conflict, threat, fear, and danger, or patterns of avoiding these signals altogether. These are two extremes that, absence a true threat, severely limit the possibilities available to you in each and every moment. When you no longer reside in fear or the avoidance of fear, you'll begin to align with creativity, connection, and flow.

It's important to begin to notice what you're orienting toward and if it's supporting you in your healing. The exercise below will introduce the practice of mindfully orienting to your surroundings to help facilitate a felt sense of safety. Orienting is an embodied practice. The only way to know if you feel safe in your skin is by listening to the signals your body's giving you. This is where the vagus nerve comes in.

Orienting Toward Safety and the Vagus Nerve

The vagus nerve is essential in helping calm you after perceived or imagined threats activate the fight-flight-freeze response. A perceived threat is when you believe there's an actual threat, even though there may not be. If there is a threat, you'll want to take action to make yourself as safe as possible. An imagined threat refers to when you remember some aspect of past trauma as though it were happening now or when you worry that something bad will happen in the future. An imagined threat will take your body into the fight-flight-freeze response just as a perceived threat will. When this happens on a regular basis, it creates an overly activated nervous system, which is not good for your health and well-being.

Beginning in the brainstem just behind your ears, the vagus nerve travels down each side of the neck, across the chest, and down through the abdomen. It networks the brain with the stomach, intestines, lungs, heart, spleen, liver, kidneys, and the nerves involved in eye contact, speech, facial expressions, and the ability to tune in to other's voices. You'll learn more about the important role the vagus nerve plays in chapters 2 and 8. The next exercise will introduce you to a simple way to calm your vagus nerve.

PRACTICE: Focus on What You See

Your eyes have a direct connection to your vagus nerve. If you mindfully orient to your environment, slowly turning your head and neck all the way from side to side as you take in your surroundings, you'll alert an activated vagus nerve that there's no present danger, that it's safe to begin to relax. This is important because to do the work that will help you heal, you'll need to be in a fairly calm state.

- Scan your body to notice how you're feeling. Is there any tension, stress, or anxiety present?

- Now slowly turn your head to one side as far as you can while scanning your surroundings.

- Slowly, as if in slow motion, turn your head to the other side as far as your neck will rotate while continuing to take in your surroundings.

- What do you notice as you slowly scan the room or environment? Where does your attention go?

- Repeat this two more times.

- Take note of how you feel in your body after orienting to your environment.

- Jot down any observations or insights that arise after doing this practice.

_____

_____

_____

If you were feeling calm to begin with, you may not notice any shift. If however, you were feeling anxious or overwhelmed, you may notice yourself beginning to calm down. We'll delve more into the practice of mindfully orienting to your surroundings to help facilitate a felt sense of safety in chapter 3. Now we'll transition to focusing on your breath.

The Importance of Conscious Breath

We take life-giving breaths twelve or so times a minute, every minute of every day, yet many of us never pause to bring conscious awareness to how we're breathing. We often underestimate and underappreciate the impact our breath has on our health and well-being. The physical benefits of conscious breathing have been well documented and, according to author and professor Christine Caldwell (2018), include:

"...improving immune function; regulating arousal; decreasing sinus problems; balancing hormones, enzymes, and neurotransmitters; stabilizing blood gases; increasing vitality;

promoting digestion, circulation, and proper organ function; facilitating waste metabolism; aligning posture; decreasing muscle tension; and increasing motility and mobility. These physical effects can in turn be seen as having profound influence on psychological well-being, particularly in the area of mood, the reduction of negative emotion and increase of positive emotion, emotional regulation, and the capacity for social engagement" (68).

So, what does this have to do with surviving sexual trauma? Unfortunately, as the result of trauma or an insecure attachment to your primary caregiver in early childhood, you may have developed breathing patterns that were adaptive at the time but are not healthy in the long run. For instance, you may have a habitually shallow breathing pattern that only fills your upper lungs, or you might hold onto your breath longer than healthy, both arising from a fear pattern. This is because restraining the breath or breathing shallowly can hold back unwelcome emotions, such as shame and fear. This causes constriction in your thorax and stomach, which further inhibits the breath.

Since these patterns likely developed in response to fear, it can be triggering to introduce change. For this reason, it's important to go slowly with breathwork and to stop if you feel dizzy, dissociated, disoriented, headachy, or triggered. Be very cautious and work with a therapist when possible if you suffer from asthma, emphysema, seizures, heart problems, migraines, diabetes, dissociative symptoms, or anger management issues. Do not push yourself when experimenting with breathwork.

Ultimately you want to cultivate relaxed, balanced breathing, with inhalation and exhalation roughly the same length. Inhaling activates your sympathetic nervous system, which is responsible for exertion and increased nervous system arousal (including the fight-flight-freeze response). Exhaling generally takes little effort and activates your parasympathetic nervous system, which is responsible for relaxation (rest and digest). Habitual shallow breath or underbreathing is often associated with depression and avoidance behaviors, while overbreathing is associated with anxiety and panic attacks.

Conscious breath can become an entry point to awareness of your bodily sensations, emotions, and memories. A breathing practice can help clear the body-mind, encouraging higher states of consciousness to emerge and nourishing your highest self.

Many people in our culture tend to suck in their abdomens. Some feel shame or embarrassment about the appearance of their bellies and suck them in to try to make them look smaller. We've been taught that it looks trim and attractive to keep our bellies tense, yet this results in physical and emotional rigidity and restriction. This feeling may be so familiar that you don't even notice it! In addition, your abdomen is a very vulnerable area of your body, with no bones to shield and protect the underlying organs. If you're a sexual assault survivor, tensing your belly may feel like protection or may be an attempt to help you resist uncomfortable feelings and sensations altogether.

Think about when you would naturally suck in your gut. Imagine someone you know walking up behind you unexpectedly. Try making the sound of being startled by surprise—it's a quick inhalation.

Did you notice how as you made the sound, your stomach automatically pulled inward? Tensing and sucking in the abdomen is part of the fight-flight response. Why should we all be encouraged to walk around sucking in our abdomens when it creates a permanent fear-startle pattern (Linden 2004)?

The muscles of the abdomen and pelvic floor form the core of the body, the center of movement and balance. Holding tension in these areas makes it impossible to ground, relax, or move freely and comfortably. During the process of breathing, the diaphragm, located just beneath the lungs, contracts and pulls down, allowing air to be sucked into the lungs. As it relaxes and moves back upward, the air is expelled. When the diaphragm pushes down, everything in the abdomen region is displaced outward, primarily to the front, but also to the sides and back. Infants naturally breathe this way, and people of all ages often shift to an abdominal breath once they fall asleep fully relaxed, but this is not how most adults in our culture breathe as they're going about their day (Linden 2004). I invite you to become aware of your breath.

PRACTICE: Belly Breaths

Abdominal breaths slow your breathing and calm the vagus nerve, supporting your sense of feeling safely embodied. It's helpful to practice belly breaths as part of your healing, but don't push yourself when experimenting with breathwork. It's best to wear comfortable clothing—if your clothes are tight, your muscles will tense up to fight the pressure.

- Begin by inviting your abdomen and pelvic floor (hips and muscles of the pelvis) to soften and relax. If you're not able to relax, it's okay; you can still try the rest of the exercise.

- Place your hands on your abdomen. Visualize breathing into your hands, letting the air fall gently down into your belly.

- Invite your lower abdomen to gently inflate with your inhalation and gently deflate with your exhalation. It may help to visualize a balloon filling with air on the inhalation, then letting the air release on the exhalation.

- Keep your focus on your abdomen for a minimum of ten to fifteen breaths to find your rhythm and pace.

- How did it feel to breathe this way?

_____

_____

_____

If you're used to sucking in your abdomen, breathing in this more relaxed manner may feel strange. You may even feel uncomfortable breathing this way until you get used to it. If you're having trouble, you can lie down and place a small stone or other object on your belly to see the gentle upward movement of the inhalation. You can practice the belly breath anywhere; just remember to keep your belly the focal point of the breath. I recommend setting a reminder on your phone to do several belly breaths every couple of hours while at work (if your job allows). It's a good way to get a little self-care into your day.

PRACTICE: Coming into Safety

The "Coming into Safety" (CIS) practice (you can call this practice Coming into Presence if the word *safety* triggers you) puts it all together: grounding, calming the vagus nerve, and conscious breath. When you begin to feel anxious, overwhelmed, or triggered, stop what you're doing for a few minutes and practice these steps. Your nervous system will begin to relax as you move out of hyperarousal. It's important to practice the steps when you feel calm so they're available to you when you're feeling anxious, overwhelmed, or fearful. You can find a copy of the CIS steps at http://newharbinger.com/46509.

Ground

- Push your legs into the ground. Feel the strength of the muscles in your legs as you engage them. Feel your feet making contact with the ground and the Earth welcoming and supporting you.

- Now relax the muscles of your legs while you wiggle your toes.

- Repeat.

- This helps you come into your body and begin to feel supported.

Orient

- Slowly turn your head and neck as far as you can from side to side three times. Take in your surroundings, noticing if you're safe.

- This helps inform your nervous system that there's no real threat present; you can now begin to relax the fight-flight response.

- If you're not safe, do whatever you need to do to protect yourself: leave the room, call for help, find an ally, call a friend.

Belly Breaths

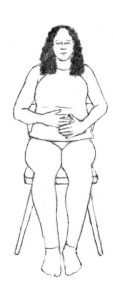

- Take slow deep breaths as you relax your belly, giving it permission to soften as you inhale. Gently let go of the breath, releasing as much air as possible without strain.

- When you inhale, the belly, ribcage, and shoulders should expand slightly, making room for the breath as the diaphragm moves downward and the lungs fill.

- It may help to imagine there's a balloon in your belly that fills up with each inhalation.

- This breath nourishes your entire being.

Soothing Touch

- Tenderly place your hands on your heart or belly, or give yourself a hug, as you remind yourself, "In this moment I am safe, I'm okay, I'm safe, I'm okay, I'm safe" or "In this moment I am present, I'm okay, I'm present."

- This touch soothes your nervous system and calms fearful thoughts.

Optional: A (new) script for when you're triggered by trauma. Reminding yourself that there's nothing wrong with you, that it's just your nervous system reacting to what it mistook for a signal of danger, disrupts negative thought patterns and helps you fully inhabit the present. Words of affirmation and compassion can further comfort you. Here's a sample script you can use to inspire this conversation with yourself.

This is my body-mind not realizing I'm safe. A painful traumatic memory may have been triggered, causing my body to react as though I'm in danger. Now, in this moment, as I ground, orient, and center myself, I know that I'm safe. I breathe deeply as I take this in, creating and embodying a new script, "I am safe, I'm healing." I gift myself the kindness and compassion I give to those I love. I am of value. I'm empowered.

The depth of safety you feel has a direct correlation to the depth of your healing. Introducing a grounding practice into your daily life is essential as you begin to learn how to come back into presence whenever your nervous system is activated. The "Coming into Safety" steps will support you in developing a foundation of being held by the Earth, supported by your breath, and feeling safe enough to enter and inhabit (if only for a time) the present moment. Go easy on yourself and be gentle, but do practice. This will gradually help cultivate a mind-body realization that the traumatic event has ended. It's now a part of your past, and you are safe in this moment.

CHAPTER 2

Understanding Your Body's Responses, Cultivating Mindfulness and Self-Compassion

You're now aware that you've been experiencing feelings and behaviors that developed in response to trauma. Your body is still trying to protect you, unfortunately in ways that cause continuing distress. Because the challenge is as deep as your body's wiring, it's highly beneficial to understand the ways your nervous system responds to threat. This chapter gives an overview of that. As you read, don't worry about memorizing words; just take in what you can. The exercises will help you break it down.

It's Not You, It's Your Nervous System

Your body's nervous system is amazing. It can automatically detect what's in your environment, always assessing and responding to cues of safety, danger, or life threat. This is called "neuroception" and occurs automatically and unconsciously originating from the most primitive part of your brain, the brainstem. The term is part of polyvagal theory, which says that our actions are automatic and adaptive in the service of survival (Porges 2011). Essentially, before your brain can make meaning of an experience, your autonomic nervous system has already assessed the environment and begun to respond.

There are two main branches of your autonomic nervous system: the sympathetic and parasympathetic. Located in the middle part of your spinal cord, the sympathetic branch prepares you for action and to defend, protect, or withdraw, and respond to cues of danger. It instigates the defense strategies associated with the fight-flight response. There are two pathways of the parasympathetic branch—the ventral vagal system and the dorsal vagal system—which travel within the vagus nerve (explained in chapter 1). "Ventral" refers to the front side, and "dorsal" refers to the back, so we're talking about the front and back of the brain stem (Porges 2011).

The ventral vagal pathway responds to cues of safety and supports feelings of calm and connection. It links your nervous system's regulation of your face and heart to form the social engagement system, which is associated with a receptive state that enables you to interact with others. Conversely, the dorsal vagal pathway responds to signs of extreme danger and is associated with shutdown behaviors, dissociative experiences, freezing, and fainting (Porges 2011; Siegel 2012). If you feel numb or frozen, the dorsal vagal circuit is running the show.

You fluctuate between these three autonomic states throughout the day: ventral vagal, sympathetic, and dorsal vagal. You can dip a little into each state in a healthy way. For instance, if you're feeling empathy or compassion for a friend, your ventral vagal system is activated. When you're working out or engaged in a stimulating conversation, you dip into the sympathetic system. The dorsal vagal system can initiate a blissful state during yoga or meditation, for example, and is responsible for your body's relaxed immobility at the end of the day when you fall into a deep sleep.

Your nervous system's ability to be flexible as it shifts from one state to another is what's important here. Learning to bring awareness to which state you're in and applying the tools, found throughout this book, that support you in moving toward ventral vagal when your nervous system has moved deep into sympathetic or dorsal vagal will help you meet this goal. Eventually the transitions will become less jarring and disruptive as you engage with the state rather than being controlled by it. The following table is a compilation of survivors' responses when deep into each of the three patterns and can help you recognize some of the biological changes taking place as you move in and out of these states.

Potential Feelings and Beliefs Associated with Each Autonomic State

Autonomic State / Pattern	Example Responses
Ventral Vagal: *Safety* *calm, social, connected*	"I feel joyful. Open, clear-headed, wanting to engage with the world." "Calm, clear, confident, in the flow, chill. It will all work out. I'm okay." "Conversational, productive, honest, appreciative, the world is fun." "There is color, life, happiness. I feel seen. I can create." "Reveling in life, the world feels delightful, magical, hopeful." "The world feels welcoming, trustworthy, and awe-inspiring."
Sympathetic: *Fight or flight* *danger, mobilized, action-taking*	"Blurry, frazzled, jumpy, paranoid, unsafe, hijacked." "Activated, aggressive, looking for escape routes to gain control." "Ready for action, alert, wanting to move or do something, prepare." "Nothing is right. I don't want to see anyone. I may be disrespectful." "The world is chaotic. What's wrong with me? Out of sync." "The world is harsh. Resources are scarce. Dangerous, angry."
Dorsal Vagal: *Freeze* *life-threat, immobilized, shut down, collapsed*	"Down, checked-out, hiding inside my own body, unloved, unsafe." "Glazed. I'm insignificant. The world is unsafe." "Listless, hopeless." "I don't want to talk to anyone. I want to cry, shut down, hide." "Numbness in extremities, stillness, breathless." "Waiting for any outcome." "The world is narrowed, muted, and viscous."

PRACTICE: **Recognizing Which Pattern You're In**

On your healing journey, it's very helpful to be able to identify when you're in one state or another. This exercise is inspired by Deb Dana's (2018) mapping autonomic profiles from the book *The Polyvagal Theory in Therapy*. To better identify which autonomic pattern you're in, take some time to reflect. Then write down what sensations and emotions you're feeling and your beliefs about yourself, others, and the world when you're in each state. Feel free to choose from the preceding examples and come up with your own.

To more easily identify each state, give it a new name if you'd like. A few of my favorites have been "Winnie the Pooh, Piglet, and Eeyore"; "Oceanic Galactic Cosmic Flow, Volcanic, and Concrete Heavy"; "Jazz, Metal, and Emo."

Ventral Vagal

Safety. Associated with social engagement, feeling calm and connected.

Your name for this state:

_____

I feel:

_____

_____

Thoughts and beliefs about myself:

_____

_____

Thoughts and beliefs about others:

_____

_____

Thoughts and beliefs about the world:

_____

_____

Sympathetic

The fight-or-flight response. The nervous system's reaction to a real or perceived danger. Associated with mobilization and action.

Your name for this state:

_____

I feel:

_____

_____

Thoughts and beliefs about myself:

_____

_____

Thoughts and beliefs about others:

_____

_____

Thoughts and beliefs about the world:

_____

_____

Dorsal Vagal

The freeze response. The nervous system's reaction to a real or perceived life-threat. Associated with immobilization, and a numb or collapsed feeling.

Your name for this state:

_____

I feel:

_____

_____

Thoughts and beliefs about myself:

_____

_____

Thoughts and beliefs about others:

_____

_____

Thoughts and beliefs about the world:

_____

_____

The Highs and Lows of Arousal

Now that you can identify your patterns, what they feel like, and how they influence your thoughts and beliefs, you can watch them change as you go about your life. Your autonomic nervous system fluctuates between high and low levels of arousal throughout the day. If you're doing something relaxing, such as calmly sipping a warm cup of tea, practicing a gentle form of yoga, petting your dog or cat, or winding down for sleep at the end of the day, your nervous system is in low arousal. Alertness and invigorating activities, such as exercise, playing or watching sports, and stimulating conversation, require higher arousal. When fluctuations are not extreme, your nervous system's arousal is regulated in or near the window of tolerance—your optimal arousal zone.

The "window of tolerance" refers to a calm (ventral vagal) state. When you feel safe, fluctuations within the window flow smoothly and are adaptive to whatever situation you're in, but when you feel threatened, your nervous system escalates outside of the window into hyper- or hypoarousal. Hyperarousal is your nervous system's first order of defense to prepare you to call for help and for the fight-or-flight response. If no one comes to help and the fight-flight defenses aren't an option or are unsuccessful, the body moves into hypoarousal, shutdown, collapse, or freeze. The experience of trauma can cause the autonomic nervous system to cycle up and down between hyperarousal and hypoarousal, seldom residing within the window of tolerance. The following list is adapted from Porges (2011), Schore (2012), and Stanley (2016).

Optimal autonomic nervous system arousal:

Window of tolerance: calm, relaxed, connected to self or others

Too much autonomic nervous system arousal:

High arousal: anger, fear, anxiety, stress

Hyperarousal: panic, terror, horror, aggression

Too little autonomic nervous system arousal:

Low arousal: fatigue, withdrawal, disconnection

Hypoarousal: disembodiment, dissociation, despair

Take a little time now to think about how you've experienced these states; then complete the following statements for each.

When _____ happens, I feel _____, which

tells me I'm in a state of _____.

When _____ happens, I feel _____, which

tells me I'm in a state of _____.

When _____ happens, I feel _____, which

tells me I'm in a state of _____.

Many survivors are hypervigilant, continually scanning their surroundings for cues of danger, easily startled, and jumpy. Fixed patterns can develop that strengthen your ability to perceive danger and life threat through your senses and bodily sensations. If you've been exposed to real or perceived danger for extended periods of time, such as repeated childhood trauma, assault, ongoing harassment, or oppression, your nervous system's activation may be pervasive. So, if for example, a friend or coworker unjustly criticizes you, rather than responding with a little defensiveness, your nervous system might move into hyperarousal with explosive anger (fight) or hypoarousal, leaving you unable to respond feeling numb or frozen. The problem with fixed patterns is that they may, or may not, reflect the actual circumstances.

Your body is not meant to sustain these extremes of defensive fixed patterns. The hypothalamus, located in the lower region of the brain, coordinates the autonomic nervous system and the activity of the pituitary, which is responsible for physiological homeostasis (body temperature, thirst, hunger, etc.), and is involved in emotional activity and sleep.

Along with the sympathetic nervous system, your hypothalamus activates your adrenal-cortisol system, which is responsible for your stress response. When you're in an ongoing state of high arousal, the chronic adrenaline and cortisol flow can send toxins surging through your veins, creating a stress response that strains your immune system, bones, organs, and muscles (Stanley 2016). Over time, if you don't take the steps to turn off a stressor, your window of tolerance narrows.

The good news is your brain is resilient and adaptable to change and healing no matter your age. The brain's continued ability to learn and grow is referred to as neuroplasticity. Mindfulness is one of many practices you'll soon learn to support the growth of new neural pathways that will strengthen your connection to ventral vagal calm.

Everything I've shared so far in this chapter illustrates how your body transforms depending on the autonomic state you're in. This in turn influences how you experience yourself, others, and the world. Neuroception, the detection of risk outside of awareness, happens so instantaneously that it precedes perception. In other words, the autonomic state you're in precedes and influences the story you tell yourself. With the awareness you're gaining now and will gain in the following exercises, you can begin to break patterns of unpredictable, extreme, or prolonged autonomic highs and lows—a positive step toward regulating your nervous system as you heal from trauma.

Common Physical Responses to the Three Autonomic States

Ventral Vagal *Safety* *calm, social, connected*	**Results in:** Reduced heart rate Activated facial muscles Increased eye contact Increased vocal rhythm and intonation Ability to hear the midrange of the human voice Stimulated digestion
Sympathetic *Fight or flight* *danger, mobilized, action-taking*	Increased heart rate Shallow breath Blood rushes away from the prefrontal cortex to the limbs Dilation of the eyes Ability to hear extreme high and low frequency Body is on alert, hypervigilant Increased pain tolerance, slowed digestion
Dorsal Vagal *Freeze* *life-threat, immobilized, shut down, collapsed*	Decreased heart rate and respiration Flat facial affect Vacant eyes Partial or full immobilization Reduced blood flow May be unable to think clearly Dissociation; feeling numb, spaced-out, or nauseous

PRACTICE: Mapping Your State

This exercise is a timeline meant to bring awareness to how your autonomic nervous system is fluctuating throughout the day. Remember some fluctuation is natural; however, trauma survivors often experience extremely high or low arousal when in sympathetic (fight or flight) or dorsal vagal (freeze) an unhealthy and uncomfortable amount of time. Filling out the following worksheet will help you recognize the situations and behaviors of others that result in your nervous system neurocepting danger. Many clients report similar feelings to what one survivor shared, "Understanding that I'm moving between these three things, made it feel better."

Begin by noticing which state you're in when you wake up. Then jot down your thoughts and feelings, and what you feel in your body next to the appropriate state on the left. Throughout the day, each time you have a recognizable shift, fill in the time at the top of the sheet and again note your feelings, sensations, thoughts, and what preceded this shift (trigger) across from the designated autonomic state. You can access a downloadable copy for tracking multiple days as well as an example completed worksheet at http://newharbinger.com/46509.

Time of Day: _____ | _____ | _____

Ventral Vagal Safety Calm, social, connected				
Sympathetic Fight or flight Danger, mobilized, action-taking				
Dorsal Vagal Freeze life-threat, immobilized, shutdown, collapsed				

After tracking and graphing your autonomic nervous state for a few days, take some time to reflect on your responses. Do you notice any patterns? For instance, do you wake up in the same state every day? Does a coworker or friend tend to trigger a certain state? You might notice you get easily triggered when you're overwhelmed or sleep deprived. Write these observations down.

_____

_____

_____

_____

_____

For now, just bring awareness to your patterns without judgment, knowing that your autonomic nervous system is doing what it has evolved to do.

Why Your Body Responded the Way It Did

Now that you have some understanding of the autonomic nervous system, you can begin to appreciate and develop compassion for why you reacted the way you did. Everything your body-mind did was a normal reaction to abnormal circumstances. Yet, sexual assault survivors are often misunderstood and judged for what they did or did not do during and following the trauma. It's easy for people to say they would have fought or tried to escape if it hasn't happened to them (and they're unaware of how the body responds to trauma). Most survivors are even harder on themselves, experiencing deep feelings of guilt and shame for not having done something differently preceding, during, or after the assault. This is a tragic mirroring of society's victim-blaming and victim-shaming that adds yet another layer of pain to an already open and raw physical, psychological, and soul wounding.

For survivors of sexual assault, there was no way to escape or flee, no one to help, and little or no possibility of overpowering the perpetrator. When the sympathetic fight-flight response was unsuccessful, your body may have neurocepted (your autonomic nervous system assessed the environment and began to respond before your brain could fully understand what was happening) that the best option for survival was dorsal vagal shutdown. The freeze response, also referred to as "tonic immobility," is an involuntary physiological response.

It's important to understand that if you froze, your inability to act was not your fault. It was your nervous system doing what it has biologically evolved to do. It shut down as the last order of defense in an attempt to keep you alive. While this may seem counterintuitive, it makes sense when we look to nature. When an animal is being hunted in the wild by another, with little or no chance of escape, it may collapse and freeze. It instinctually plays dead to avoid becoming prey. When the hungry animal comes across the collapsed and frozen animal, it usually mistakes the prey for dead (remember the heart rate slows way down in dorsal vagal) and moves on because instinctually it knows to only eat fresh kill (Levine 1997). Along the same lines, in some cases, our chances of survival are greater when we don't fight back.

You don't have to be aware of fearing for your life to move into a freeze response. It's beyond your conscious control. It's clear from both my personal and clinical experience that when you know the perpetrator, the likelihood of freezing increases. Confusion, overwhelm, shock, and grief are immediate when a coworker, friend, partner, or family member with whom you have some level of trust betrays that trust in the worst possible way.

A few weeks after my nineteenth birthday, I was raped by someone I thought was a friend while the young man I'd just started dating sat in the next room, unbeknownst to me until that moment, after having set me up for the assault. In shock with tears streaming down my face, I repeatedly said no but was unable to fight. The immense betrayal sent me into tonic immobility. Two years later, I was running in a suburban neighborhood when I was assaulted by a stranger. This time, my nervous system remained in sympathetic as I fought for my life, and while traumatized, I averted the rape. Months later while traveling for work, I again found myself betrayed by an acquaintance whom I thought was a friend, an employer who was in possession of my plane ticket home. Again, I said no, and again my body froze as he raped me. In each situation my body neurocepted the state that offered my best chance of survival. Like mine, your body responded in the best way possible under the circumstances you were in. The body as an organism will always go toward survival.

Can you relate to any of what I shared? How did your body respond?

_____

_____

_____

_____

_____

While it's true that your body develops patterns of responses, when you include your body in the healing process, you can generate change in these patterns.

Mindfulness: Growing New Neural Pathways to Take You into Calm

Albert Einstein reportedly said, "Perhaps the fundamental freedom that anyone possesses is the choice of where to put their attention." Neuroscience has shown that the brain changes in response to what you focus your attention on. Whatever you repeat—good, bad, or indifferent—is strengthened. In other words, if you think depressed, anxious, and fearful thoughts over and over again, you fire brain circuits that strengthen the neural pathways that bring you to feelings of depression, anxiety, and fear. Fortunately, the brain is malleable, and you can, with time, create new neural pathways that lead to feelings of happiness, calm, and safety.

This knowledge has contributed to the popularity of mindfulness practices that cultivate awareness of present-moment experience with intention and without judgment or interpretation. A vast amount of research on mindfulness indicates a greater ability to manage and tolerate emotions; an increased ability to effectively cope with stress; increased attention, focus, and concentration; improved empathy and insight; the promotion of healthy immune functioning; and increased growth of regulatory and integrative regions of the brain. I suggest twelve minutes a day or thirty minutes three times a week of mindful awareness or a meditation practice that includes self-compassion to help generate these changes.

Mindfulness can be practiced in two ways: informal, which is bringing present-moment awareness to whatever activity you're engaged in (eating, walking, chores, communicating), or formal, also known as directed, which is taking time out on a regular basis, usually daily, to intentionally select elements of present-moment experience to focus on (breath, body sensations, senses, mantras, prayer).

Mindfulness practice can seem pretty simple and straightforward but doesn't come easy for many survivors who consciously or unconsciously avoid feeling present by disconnecting from their body, numbing out, or dissociating. This pattern begins with the dorsal vagal's immobilizing survival response—it wasn't safe to be fully present during the trauma. If this is the case for you, mindfulness can be challenging at first. Take it slowly. You can start with staying present for thirty seconds, then work up to one minute, and continue at a pace that is comfortable for you with the goal of eventually getting to twelve minutes of daily practice. If you become overwhelmed, change your focus from whatever it's been on, such as your breath, to something neutral, like your hands (unless they're a trigger for you) or an innocuous object in your surroundings.

Mindfulness strengthens your ability to choose where you want to focus your attention rather than feeling under the control of your thoughts. As you practice, don't get discouraged if your mind wanders to repetitive thoughts of the past (known as ruminations) or future worries. Just acknowledge them and then gently come back to the present. The more you try to control your ruminations and worries, the more invasive they'll become. Allow the thought, and then let it fade away without judgment or resistance. It can help to imagine an image of the past or future thought spelled out above you, rising up like a balloon floating further and further away or just dissolving into thin air. The moment you realize you're not present is the very moment you become present.

PRACTICE: Sight, Sound, Taste, Touch, Smell

This mindfulness practice can quickly ground you in the present. Simply bring awareness to what you're sensing and feeling in the moment, focusing on one of your five senses, without interpretation or judgment.

- **Sight**. Look around and notice what you're drawn to. Focus on it, taking in every detail. For example, you might notice what direction the light's coming from, how it reflects from its surface, what colors you see, how they change with the light, and the surface or texture of the object.

- **Sound**. Notice the sounds in your environment. You may find there are several you've been filtering out. Focus on listening to one at a time. You might notice rhythms, tones, pitches, and after isolating and exploring each, the symphony of all of the sounds combined.

- **Taste**. Take a bite of food or a sip of a beverage and notice what you taste. For instance, you might notice if it's bitter, salty, sour, sweet, warm, or cool. Swoosh it around your mouth and observe which taste buds are awakened. You might try tasting the air on your tongue or simply noticing how your mouth tastes.

- **Touch**. Notice how your clothing feels against your skin, the pressure of your feet on the floor, the weight of your body on the surface you're sitting, what textures you feel, the temperature on your skin, how the air is circulating, or a breeze.

- **Smell**. Again, isolate any scents you can pick up on in your environment. You might explore the subtler aromas after taking in those that are hard to miss. If you have access to essential oils, try isolating each herb in a blend.

How to Fit Mindfulness into a Busy Day

Psychologist and author Tara Brach (2020) said, "I'm going to come into stillness and pay attention every day no matter what. It doesn't matter how long or where. All that matters is that I consciously pause and dedicate a few moments to be here in this moment. It's a gift to the soul to have that rhythm, like the rhythm of the earth turning, of coming home every day." One of the wonderful things about mindfulness practice is that you can "come home" most anytime and anywhere. In informal practice, anything you're able to do with undivided attention while remaining present, such as eating, going for a walk or walking a dog, washing dishes or other chores, showering, or bathing, can be a form of mindfulness. The following are suggestions for your informal practice:

- Give the experience your full, undivided attention.

- Practice nonstriving.

- Slow the process down.

- Observe the body-mind with curiosity.

- Suspend judgment.

- Make compassion for others and yourself a part of the practice.

Many of my clients combine practices such as "Coming into Safety," "Toe Tapping," and the "Self-Compassion Steps" (below) to make up their twelve minutes of daily mindfulness practice. You can also try a technique called progressive muscle relaxation, which can help generate a shift toward ventral vagal calm and keep you from being stuck in a stress pattern. Download the instructions at http://newharbinger.com/46509.

If you have a job that allows, I suggest setting the timer on your phone for every couple of hours as a reminder to check in with yourself, take a few belly breaths, and center and ground yourself, becoming aware of your internal experience in the here and now without judgment. In addition to reducing stress, practicing presence will gradually help dissolve the pain of the past.

Why Self-Compassion Is So Important

According to psychologist and author Kristin Neff (2020), "Self-compassion is holding your pain with love." Sadly, many have developed a deep-rooted belief that they're not good enough, not worthy of love, even from themselves. Turning against ourselves is fairly universal and often takes the form of a subtle "something is wrong with me" feeling. Sexual trauma can heighten these painful beliefs, which may have first taken root at a very tender age when you were dependent on your parent(s) or primary caregiver for your survival.

When infants and young children don't get their basic needs met, their brains can't yet comprehend that their caregiver could have both good moods and bad and be both loving and dismissive, rejecting, or in some cases even cruel. Their health is dependent on the belief they'll be protected and cared for. When the person they love and are dependent on doesn't meet their needs, which can range from recurrent misattunement without repair to the deep wounds of neglect and abuse, the vulnerable infant or young child begins to embody a sense that they're flawed. So begins the turning against one's self.

It's from this wounded place that survivors often confuse sexual trauma as evidence of their lack of worth: "If I were more together, smarter, successful, more or less attractive…this wouldn't have happened to me." I was able to learn this, and you need to know it too: nothing about you or your choices justify what happened to you. These and all other negative habitual thoughts are at the root of much of your suffering.

Fortunately, your brain and body are capable of forming new patterns of thought and concurrent physiological actions. You don't have to continue turning against yourself with what really amounts to self-inflicted violence. What's needed is to begin a practice, like the next one, of giving your adult self the kindness and compassion you were unable to give yourself as a child. Extending compassion to yourself may feel awkward or even difficult at first. As with learning any new skill, it takes practice, but what a worthy investment you are!

Self-compassion generates self-acceptance, appreciation, confidence, and well-being. When you recognize your intrinsic value, you relax and settle into yourself. It's the antidote to the collapsed posture and freeze of shame. Everyone has failures. They're part of how we learn and evolve, but unlike self-esteem, self-compassion doesn't relate to your performance or some arbitrary measure of success. Self-compassion is never about pity, perfection, or narcissism; instead it's about fostering acceptance, awareness, accountability, and growth. Practicing self-compassion creates a foundation of warmth where kindness to yourself and others can blossom.

We can learn to stop and catch our thoughts as we begin to turn against ourselves. Kristin Neff is a pioneer in the field of self-compassion research, I highly recommend her self-compassion quiz at http://www.self-compassion.org. She teaches that it's essential to embrace your suffering with kindness, to recognize that failure, imperfection, and suffering are part of our shared humanity. Neff identified three elements of self-compassion: self-kindness versus self-judgment, common humanity versus isolation, and mindfulness versus over-identification. The following practice incorporates all three and is inspired by Kristin Neff and Chris Garber's (2018) Self Compassion Break exercise (10–11).

PRACTICE: Finding a Soothing Touch

Humans need touch. Babies and young children cannot survive without it, and adults continue to benefit from it. Welcomed touch is calming and regulating to your nervous system, even if it's you doing the touching. This is why "Coming into Safety" and the "Self-Compassion Steps" (below) practices use touch. Before you begin the "Self-Compassion Steps," take a few minutes to explore where you feel the most comforted by your touch; be sure that your hands are relaxed and your touch is gentle.

- Try placing both hands over your heart, feel your heart, and let your hands soften into it. Take several slow deep breaths while you notice if this feels soothing and calming, or not.

- Next move one hand to your stomach and leave one over your heart, take a few deep breaths, and take note of how this feels.

- Now place both hands on your stomach and notice how this feels.

- Try placing both hands on your chin cupping your jaw and checks.

- Bring both hands down, wrists crossing over one another at your heart center with your fingers resting just above or on your collarbone.

- Finally give yourself a hug. You might try hugging up near your shoulders or lower down near your elbows, whatever feels best to you.

Which placement felt most supportive to you?

_____

This is the touch you'll bring into step 3 of the "Self-Compassion Steps" that follow.

PRACTICE: Self-Compassion Steps

Sadly, the more you're in need self-compassion, the less likely you are to stop and be kind to yourself. This is usually because it's hard to receive the compassion. You may struggle to take it in due to harsh judgments and internalized shame. Just as with the previous exercises, this is a muscle you'll grow with practice. With time, rather than turning against yourself, a form of violence turned inward, you'll become your own best ally. These steps are also available at http://newharbinger.com/46509.

1. **This hurts.** Acknowledge that you're experiencing pain. It may be in the form of self-defeating thoughts, challenging emotions, betrayal, loss, challenging circumstances, or physical pain. Simply bring awareness to the fact that you're hurting or suffering in some way.

2. **Others are hurting.** Now, bring awareness to the fact that you are not alone in your pain. You're not flawed because you're suffering. Vulnerability, fragility, and suffering are part of the human condition. Try to accept and honor your humanness. Don't confuse this with shaming yourself for being in pain with statements like, "I shouldn't feel this way when others have it so much worse." Simply acknowledge that you are not alone.

3. **Offer kind words with touch.**

   a. Imagine that a friend or child you love came to you experiencing the same hurt. You might also imagine yourself as a child feeling this pain. Take a moment and think of what you would say to comfort them. What kind words of support and encouragement would you offer?

b.   Once you find the words, gently place your hands where you felt most soothed in the previous exercise then say the same words to yourself. Notice if you're able to take them in.

4. **Take it in.** Sometimes we can't receive the kind words. Chris Garber calls this backdraft, a term from firefighting. It refers to what happens if you open a door and there's a raging fire on the other side. Explosive flames come rushing out into the available oxygen. If you haven't received a lot of compassion in your life or haven't felt worthy of the compassion you've received, the pain in your heart can feel like the flames rushing out. With practice, this will subside.

    a.   If you're having trouble taking in the kind words, notice what's preventing you. It might be a strong inner critic saying something like, "Yeh, but not you," or some other disparaging message, or it might be a feeling in your body, such as a tightness or shield around your heart.

    b.   Now do the steps again, bringing compassion for the feeling or thought that prevented you from taking it in. Continue this process for as many rounds as needed until you get to a point where you receive the compassion.

It's important not to forget the second step because it helps steer you away from self-pity. Practice the "Self-Compassion Steps" whenever your thoughts turn against you, when you feel emotional or physical pain, and especially when you're experiencing the debilitating collapse of shame. As author Zora Neale Hurston reportedly said, "Love makes your soul crawl out from its hiding place."

⌐ *Story:* Learning to Take in Self Compassion

It's common for those healing from sexual trauma to be too resistant or defended to take in any compassion, even from themselves. Learning to do so requires great patience and persistence. But, as Isabel learned, it can be a powerful turning point toward well-being.

Isabel came to me in her early thirties, having suffered physical abuse as a child. She was molested by a relative at age five and, like most molestation victims, was too afraid to tell anyone. In addition, her parents used a belt to discipline her on a regular basis. If she talked back or didn't tell the truth, she got the belt. If she didn't perform well in school, she got the belt. If she cried out in pain, the beating would begin all over again. As an adult, Isabel continued to suffer ongoing racial and sexual cultural oppression, which reinforced deep-seated painful feelings of unworthiness.

When Isabel first came to see me, her nervous system was highly unregulated, cycling between hyper- and hypoarousal, causing her to vacillate between intense feelings of rage and painful depressive lows. A couple of months into our work, she was able to stay grounded for longer periods of time resulting in less frequent dissociative symptoms, yet connecting with any sense of worthiness was still challenging. As I taught Isabel the self-compassion steps, her nervous system began to shift into dorsal vagal immobilization. Her shoulders slumped forward, a palpable feeling of shame washed over her, and a tear ran down her cheek as she struggled to take it in.

As children so often do, Isabel had internalized a belief that she was unworthy of love in an attempt to make sense of all the bad things that had happened to her. Intellectually, she knew the abuse was not her fault, that she was not bad or unlovable, yet her body-mind still reacted as though this were true. As she tried to take in compassion, the pain came rushing out. I reassured her that if she stuck with the practice, eventually she'd be able to take it in. With repetition, self-compassion would become easier.

Over the next few months, I'd occasionally remind Isabel of the practice, asking her to try again, to follow the steps until she could connect with compassion. She'd begrudgingly promise to try, anticipating her usual disappointment, until one day Isabel arrived at the office standing tall and smiling as she proudly reported she'd succeeded, that she took in self-compassion. It was an important milestone in her healing that lead to many other positive shifts and ultimately to the self-acceptance that had eluded Isabel her whole life, which wouldn't have been possible without the ability to assimilate and integrate self-compassion.

When Isabel ended therapy, she was using the self-compassion practice almost daily. Her nervous system was much more regulated, she knew how to work with difficult feelings, such as shame, when they arose, and she was able to connect with a genuine feeling of love and acceptance for herself.

You're making progress; keep up the good work! Next, we'll explore sensations, why they're important, and how to begin to identify, accept, and work with them.

CHAPTER 3

Sensations Are the Language
Your Body Speaks

You're making meaning through your body every moment of every day. Your thoughts and feelings express themselves through your gestures, facial expressions, eye gaze, posture, and movement. In all your interactions, as much as 95 percent of communication happens in the narrative told through your body, rather than your words. Consider what makes you feel seen and understood by another person: Is it their words alone or the fact that they're fully present, not only listening attentively but also tracking your body's subtle signals, reading its micro-movements, and responding with sensitivity to what they observe?

You cannot heal from trauma without listening to and working with the body and what it's communicating. As you may have discovered when you filled out "Recognizing Which Pattern You're In" (chapter 2), what you experience physically and what you believe mentally are intimately connected. Every aspect of physical experience is integrative in nature. This means what you physically feel has a strong influence on what you think and believe. Conversely, your thoughts, interpretations, and beliefs affect your body and what you physically feel. While your body can move without thought preceding it, every thought produces subtle or not so subtle movement within your body (Bowen 2012). An emotional pain, such as hurt, might generate a constriction or an ache in your chest or stomach. With anger, you might feel tension in your jaw, shoulders, or abdomen. This is your body communicating to you, letting you know that something needs your attention.

Why Sensations Are Important

During and after the traumatic experience, you may have disconnected from your body's sensations in an attempt to lessen the physical and emotional pain. It wasn't safe for you to be in your body, so you learned to numb or dissociate. In addition, if you didn't get your basic needs of safety and nurturing met as a child, you may feel ashamed or even repulsed by your body, reinforcing the tendency to disconnect.

A sensation is a physical feeling or perception, a bodily awareness. Just as your emotions come and go, so too do your internal sensations. Getting in touch with sensations can help you notice the subtle changes and responses that are continuously taking place, which in turn can help discharge excess energy and complete feelings and responses from the trauma that were previously blocked. Bringing your awareness to these changes and responses enhances them.

Take a few minutes now to go inward, close your eyes or bring them to a soft focus by closing them part way or looking to the peripheral. Then scan your body and notice what sensations call out to you. If you've numbed or disconnected from your bodily sensations, it can feel uncomfortable scanning your body at first. Try shifting your attention to your breath or doing "Come into Safety." When you're ready, gently open your eyes and describe what sensations you noticed.

_____

_____

_____

Was it difficult for you to get in touch with a sensation? What happened as you tried to go inward?

_____

_____

_____

One way to observe a sensation is to start with identifying what you're feeling, and then ask, "What tells me I'm feeling this way, or how do I recognize this feeling in my body?" If for example, you're feeling in connection with a loved one, nature, or something greater than yourself, you may feel a sense of warmth and expansion radiating from your heart. If you're feeling fearful, you might notice a constriction in your throat, a knot in your stomach, or a rapid heartbeat, and if you're experiencing grief, you may feel an achy, heavy, or "broken" heart.

Identify what emotion your feeling. How do you recognize the feeling in your body?

_____

_____

_____

Patterns of bodily constriction bridge your trauma to new situations and take you out of direct perceptual experience or awareness. Learning to stay present with the sensation until it begins to change is key to dissolving this constriction (Levine 2008). When you're able to observe and reduce the intensity of your sensations and emotions, you generate choice and begin to modify the overwhelming survival responses (which you explored in chapter 2).

Try not to get discouraged if at first you find it hard to connect with your body's sensations. Feeling numb, anxious, and fearful are fairly common responses when developing sensation awareness. If getting in touch with a sensation feels overwhelming, try changing your focus, perhaps to a part of your body that feels neutral or an object in your surroundings, and observing every detail as though you were going to paint a picture of it. Go slow and be gentle with yourself. Your tolerance will steadily build.

Types of Sensations

There are several types of sensory neurons. Many are categorized in the list below. It's not necessary to memorize this list. The aim is to become aware of moving back and forth between these three types of sensory neurons, ultimately cultivating a balanced awareness.

Proprioception

- Sensations of body position, movement, balance, and orientation in space.
- Location in relationship to the outer world and from one part of the body to another.
- Located in the inner ear, around various joints, and within muscles.
- Linked to focus and sustained attention.

Exteroception

- Sensations that pick up stimuli from the outside world.
- Usually located near or on the surface of the body.
- Sensors in the nose, eyes, ears, and skin.
- Monitoring borders and tracking your body's relationship to the space around it.

Interoception

- Senses that gather data about your internal world.
- Breathing and heart rate; feeling hot or cold, hunger or thirst, sexual arousal, pain or comfort.

- Monitoring your inner well-being, metabolism, and arousal.

- Tracking inner sensations is correlated to emotional intelligence and the ability to make good decisions.

Sensations List

When healing from trauma, it's important to begin to expand your capacity to tune in to your body's wisdom. If bringing awareness to sensations is unfamiliar, referring to the sensations list below will be helpful as you learn how your body's reacting and responding to your thoughts, your perceptions, and the information you're receiving from your surroundings. Many of the words are commonly used, others not so much. Feel free to come up with some of your own as you progress through the practices. You can access a downloadable copy at http://newharbinger.com/46509.

achy	airy	animated	ascending	bloated	blocked	breathless
burning	butterflies	buzzy	calm	chills	churning	clammy
clenched	congested	constricted	cold	collapsed	cool	damp
dense	descending	dizzy	dull	effervescent	electric	empty
energized	expanding	faint	flaccid	fluid	flushed	fluttery
floaty	frozen	goosebumps	hard	heavy	hot	intense
itchy	jagged	jerky	jittery	jumbled	jumpy	knotted
light	listless	moist	moving	murky	nauseous	numb
paralyzed	pinching	pins, needles	pressure	prickly	puffy	pulsating
quaking	quivering	radiating	rigid	shaky	sharp	shivery
shudder	smooth	soft	solid	sore	space	spasms
spinning	stiff	stringy	strong	suffocating	sweaty	tense
tenuous	thick	tickly	tight	tingly	trembling	twitchy
vaporous	vibrating	warm	weak	weighty	wiggly	wobbly

PRACTICE: Safely Sensing Inward

For this practice you'll become aware of a sensation, and then stay with it for a few minutes, noticing any subtle changes that take place. Bringing awareness to these changes is most beneficial, according to trauma expert Peter Levine (2008), when you try not to "interpret, analyze, or explain what is happening. Just experience and note it" (57).

The first time you try this, see if you can find a sensation to work with that feels pleasurable, comforting, or peaceful. If the sensation you connect with is painful, bringing awareness to the pain can at first seem to increase it. If this happens, you can choose to redirect your focus to a part of your body that feels neutral, such as your hands or the tip of your nose. Don't judge yourself. It's just your body's way of telling you to be gentle and slow down. With time, it will feel less activating, and you'll grow to appreciate your body's wisdom.

- Find a comfortable quiet place to sit or lie down without distraction.

- Softly focus or close your eyes as you go inward and begin to get in touch with your breath. Make your exhalations long and slow, releasing everything that you don't need right now: your stress, distractions from the outside, anything that would keep you from paying attention to your experience.

- Watch with a sense of playful curiosity as you wait for sensations to develop or call your attention. As images, thoughts, and feelings come and go, make note of them. Then let them go. Refrain from judging what you notice as right or wrong, good or bad.

- Take your time to fully experience what sensations arise. Choose one sensation and try to stay present with it.

- If you feel fearful or overwhelmed, stop the practice and return to "Coming into Safety." After you connect with a sense of safety, try the "Self-Compassion Steps."

- Once you're able to stay with the sensation, notice how it feels. Is there pressure, tingling, pain, tension, warmth?

- Can you find an edge where it begins and ends? Does it go from inward to outward or vice versa? Does it spread, lessen, or change in any way? Stay with the sensation for several minutes.

Using the list of sensation words, describe what you experienced.

_____

_____

_____

_____

Did the sensation shift or change in any way?

_____

_____

_____

_____

Are any thoughts, emotions, images, or memories present as you describe the sensation?

_____

_____

_____

_____

The idea is to track and experience the sensation for a time, uninterrupted, to gain the realization first-hand that sensations shift, move, and eventually dissipate, which means you're not stuck. The more awareness you bring to your bodily sensations, the more comfortable you'll become with what you experience. Getting in touch with sensations can help you feel safe in your body. With time, you'll learn its language, the subtle signals it sends you, to draw on the wisdom it has to offer, and all of this will strengthen your resilience.

Finding a Sense of Internal Well-Being

A resource is someone or something that elicits, supports, and nurtures a felt sense of well-being. Resources are internal, external, or both, and can remind you of your emotional, somatic, cognitive, and spiritual strengths and positive experiences. The more resources you have, the better equipped you'll be to handle the disappointments and challenges life brings. Unfortunately, a traumatic event can cause you to lose touch with your resources, bringing about feelings of inadequacy and unworthiness. If you experienced trauma when you were young, you may have had little opportunity to develop or learn to recognize your resources. Even so, everybody and every _body_ has resources (Levine 2008).

Both internal and external resources fall into the following categories (Ogden and Fisher 2015). Circle the ones that resonate with you or that you want to cultivate. Then see if you can come up with others you already have or want to strengthen to add to the list.

Resource	Associated Gifts, Talents, Competencies, and Strengths
Relational	Deep friendships, close family members, a beloved pet, boundaries, a sense of belonging to a group, communication skills, intimacy
Somatic	Sensation awareness, grounding, belly breaths, strength/flexibility, good health, performing important physiological functions/skills
Emotional	Giving and receiving emotional support, ability to tolerate emotions, ability to communicate emotions, not being controlled by emotions
Intellectual	Objective reasoning and understanding, abstract reasoning, reading, problem solving, continued learning and growth, intellectual clarity
Psychological	A healthy sense of self, ability to reflect on one's self, feeling safe, when there's no imminent threat, nonjudgmental self-awareness
Artistic	Ability to access the creative process, to drop into a flow state, self-expression, expressive arts, design, play, spontaneity
Material	Ability to earn a comfortable wage; capacity to enjoy material things; a comfortable space; healthy time, money, and property boundaries
Spiritual	Spiritual energy or faith, meditation, prayer or chanting, gratitude, belief, reverence, a connection to something greater than oneself
Nature	Ability to connect with and feel the expansiveness and wonder of nature, tune in to all of your senses in nature, forest bathing, play

Your gifts, talents, competencies, and strengths are all resources. The most essential internal resource is awareness of your somatic sense of self. Somatic resources operate on a continuum of creative to survival in nature and are interconnected to what you're experiencing psychologically and emotionally.

Creative ———————————————————————— **Survival**

openness and flexibility   defensiveness and constriction

Here, "creativity" refers to much more than the arts. This is your system in creative flow. Creative resources help you live your full potential. Creativity is relational, is expansive, and directly engages you with the environment. Its calm or playfulness is found in ventral vagal safety. Survival tends to be internally and externally guarded and defensive. When you can't take anymore stimulation or overwhelm, your system turns to survival resources for support. Although survival resources are necessary, they're an important function that come at a price (Bowen 2012).

Your movements reveal the internal resources you've developed to make the best of what life has presented you. The wounding of sexual trauma overwhelms somatic and psychological resources, which can result in patterns of physical constriction, hyperreactivity, holding, collapse, dissociation, and more. Getting in touch with and developing new resources, according to somatic therapist and educator, Bill Bowen (2012), will help you "find and maintain a sense of inner strength, flexibility, balance, integrity, insight, and creativity" (23).

The internal and external resources available to you play a large role in determining whether or not you'll develop PTSD after sexual trauma. If, for example, Kysha came from a loving supportive family and Nina grew up in an environment of physical and emotional abuse, Nina will likely have far fewer resources available to help her cope with the trauma. She may not have a loving supportive family member or friend to reach out to console her (external). In fact, reaching out at all may be difficult (internal), and Nina may have seldom or never felt safe within her body (internal). If either is experiencing financial hardship, she may not have the funds to pay for therapy, yet Kysha may be aware of and able to reach out for help at low-fee training clinics, sliding-scale therapists, spiritual counselors, or other alternatives. Getting the immediate resources of help and support may be enough to prevent Kysha from developing PTSD. Both Kysha's and Nina's healing will include reclaiming lost resources, such as feeling safely embodied, but Nina's will also need to focus on building many new resources, including growing the capacity to feel worthy and secure enough to reach out to others for support.

You also have survival resources that helped you get through the traumatic event(s). Dissociating and the fight-flight-freeze response are examples of instinctive survival resources. Fawning, which is exaggerated affection to gain favor, is a common survival tactic and resource used among molestation victims (more on this in chapter 7). By currying favor of the perpetrator, survivors likely lessened, if ever so slightly, the intensity, degree, or frequency of abuse. But these survival resources outside of a true threat may no longer be serving you.

Which survival resources helped to get you through your trauma(s)? Let go of any self-judgment as you remember that your body was doing the best it could to keep you alive. You might have called for help, ran or tried to run, froze, fought, dissociated, or passed out.

_____

_____

_____

What are some of the internal resources that have helped you to survive since the traumatic event(s)? A few examples are determination to heal, the ability to give and receive emotional support, a yoga practice, and offering self-compassion when needed.

_____

_____

_____

What are some of the external resources that have helped you survive since the traumatic event(s), such as being in nature, a beloved pet, a therapist, or a kind friend?

_____

_____

_____

It's important to learn to recognize the many resources and competencies you've developed throughout your life. Fortunately, you can get in touch with lost resources, strengthen those that are weak, and build new ones. The following exercises will help you get in touch with an external and an internal resource.

PRACTICE: **An Object or Image of Safety**

Establishing resources can bring you a sense of comfort when sensations are too unpleasant or difficult. In this exercise you will discover or recover an *external resource*. This might be an object from nature, such as a rock, shell, or plant; a meaningful possession; an inspiring piece of art, dance, or music; or the image of a loved one, friend, or pet.

- Close or softly focus your eyes. Take a few deep yet gentle breaths. Notice yourself settling into the chair or whatever surface you're sitting or lying on.

- Think of or imagine an external resource, something that gives you a sense of comfort or is special to you.

- Choose one resource and begin to focus on it. Can you connect with some positive feelings? If not, try another resource until you find one that brings an inner smile or sense of warmth, joy, calm, or expansion.

- Once you connect with this feeling, bring your awareness to your internal sensations. What sensations tell you that you're feeling warmth, joy, calm, or expansion?

- Where is the sensation located? What shape is it? Is it moving? What else can you observe?

- Allow yourself to observe and enjoy the sensation as long as you'd like.

- When you're ready, gently bring your focus back to your surroundings.

Take some time to describe your experience and the sensations you felt. Try to be as specific as possible. You can refer to the sensations list above.

_____

_____

_____

_____

_____

_____

If your resource is something small, such as a stone, it can be soothing to carry it with you and hold it when needed, or you might take a picture of your resource for easy access on your phone. Try getting in touch with it when your nervous system begins to get activated and any time you'd like to connect with the positive sensations and feelings your resource evoked.

PRACTICE: Tapping in the Good

This is a great practice to use when you connect to a positive feeling, one that includes your thoughts, emotions, and bodily sensations. Drawn from a technique used in EMDR (eye movement desensitization and reprocessing), an evidenced-based therapy method developed by Francine Shapiro, "Tapping in the Good" uses bilateral stimulation to reinforce your resources and feel-good moments. Like mindfulness, slow bilateral tapping helps strengthen and grow neural pathways in your brain that take you to a calm, feel-good state. Along with the tapping, simply staying a little longer with the feel-good moment makes these neurons more likely to fire together in the future. So over time, you're promoting a state of calm and relaxation by staying longer with your positive moments, which can counteract a tendency for the neurons in your brain to move toward and intensify anxiety. You're literally tapping in the good feelings.

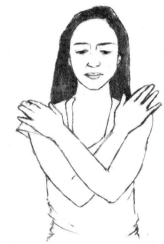

- Begin with a feel-good moment. A few examples of times to tap in are when you receive praise, when you're overcome with joy, or when you feel connected to nature. It's important you're tapping in feelings and resources that you want to strengthen.

- Place your right hand on your left shoulder and your left hand on your right shoulder.

- Gently tap your left shoulder, then tap your right, back to your left, and so on.

- Go slow, about one tap a second or slower.

- Tap seven or more times on each shoulder.

That's all there is to it! If you prefer, you can tap one thigh, forearm, or hand, and then the other, as long as you tap slowly and from one side of your body to the other as you tap in the good.

PRACTICE: A Place of Strength or Calm

The goal of this practice is to connect with a place in your body that feels safe, that lets you access a feeling of strength or calm, an *internal resource*. Understandably it can be challenging for survivors to relax or let down their guard. Learning to connect with parts of your body that feel safe or neutral can help you work with areas that are tense, easily activated, numb, disconnected, or feel more vulnerable. As you locate and work with these internal resources, you'll gradually build your tolerance to connect with all of your sensations, allowing your body's wisdom to become more fully available to you.

As with the previous practice, if you feel fearful or overwhelmed, stop the practice and return to "Coming into Safety" (chapter 1). After you shift toward ventral vagal (safety), try the "Self-Compassion

Steps" (chapter 2), and don't judge yourself. It's just your body's way of telling you to take it easy and slow down.

- Make yourself as comfortable as possible. Take a few deep yet gentle breaths. Feel your weight on whatever surface is supporting you.

- Shift your focus to your clothing touching your skin; notice how this feels. Are there other sensations you notice on the surface of your skin?

- Now drop below the surface to the muscles underneath your skin. Notice what sensations are present there. What is the temperature? Is there pressure or any movement?

- Scan for sensations all over your body. For example, perhaps you feel warmth in your heart center, butterflies in your stomach, tingling in your hands, or tension in your jaw.

- Now see if you can locate a place in your body where you feel a sense of calm or strength. Do you feel strength in your thighs, abdomen, shoulders, hands, or somewhere else?

- Do you feel your body comfortably settling? If so where?

- If you're unable to find a place in your body where you're experiencing comfort, go back to your external resource, get a clear image of it, feel into it, and then notice what happens in your body.

- Can you locate a sense of well-being? Look for the sensations that tell you this. What are they? Are you experiencing a sense of openness or spaciousness?

- Do you notice a smile or a feeling of warmth in your body? If so, stay with it and observe the sensation a little longer. You might tap in the sensation ("Tapping in the Good") of strength or calm before gently bringing your attention back to your surroundings.

These positive sensations are resources you can build upon to strengthen a sense of internal well-being. If it was challenging for you to locate an internal resource, you can come back to this exercise in a few days or when you're further along in this process, such as after chapter 5. Take a moment now to write down what you experienced.

_____

_____

_____

_____

⌐ *Story: A Safe Place*

Adriana survived an incredibly traumatic childhood. Her mother had been raped by several men, leading to an unwanted pregnancy and her resulting birth. Left to stay for months at a time with relatives, she was treated as an outcast in her small town. As an adolescent she was molested, abused, and threatened by two older teens who were supposed to be looking after her. She immigrated to the US with the promise of a high school education, only to be put to work as a nanny and maid. Adriana gathered the courage and means to leave that situation in her early twenties, but was sexually assaulted again on two occasions. Due to her immigrant status, she was understandably afraid to report these assaults.

Given this intense level of complex trauma, Adriana struggled to find an object of safety. She thought of a beloved dog, but the dog didn't belong to her, and she was no longer able to spend time with him, which made her feel sad. She liked stones and crystals but didn't connect them to a sense of safety. In fact, she didn't like the idea of choosing an object as a resource.

Then we talked about finding a peaceful place. At first nothing came to her. I knew she liked to spend time in nature and had recently been to the mountains. She began to relax as she connected to the memory. Soon she recalled that a friend had accompanied her there, and they later had a falling out, so the peaceful feeling didn't last.

I suggested she try another place in nature, perhaps somewhere she'd been to on her own. She closed her eyes, her face softened, and her body relaxed as she transported herself to a beautiful beach. Adriana took in all of the details, the vibrant colors, the sounds of waves rolling in and out on the shore, birds flying overhead, the smell of salt air, the warmth of the sun's rays on her skin, and a gentle breeze softly touching her face. Most importantly, Adriana felt safe and connected to something greater than herself.

When Adriana opened her eyes, she reported a sensation of expansion in her heart center and a feeling of deep gratitude. I asked her to stay with the sensation and feeling a little longer as she tapped them in to strengthen the calm and peaceful neural pathways being activated. After this session, she started going to the ocean more often to calm, center, ground, and nurture herself. When she couldn't get there, Adriana continued to visualize and tap into her resource to connect with an internal sense of well-being.

Rhythms of Life

Like Adriana, you can use your attention to shift your experience. All life is moved by energy. Our bodies, including our sensations, are in continual dynamic flux, alive and shifting, contracting and expanding, changing shape and intensity. The more awareness you bring to these shifts, the more apparent they'll become. By accepting the full range of sensations you experienced in relation to the traumatic event(s), you'll prompt your nervous system to restore balance.

In order to move through trauma, it's important to separate out the sensations, thoughts, images, and emotions that cause nervous system arousal. When you're able to bring awareness to and track sensations, you'll move through habitual traumatic patterning. This frees you from the grip of thoughts and images that used to cause strong and overwhelming reactions (Levine 2008).

Your nervous system naturally oscillates between states like a pendulum, contracting and expanding, then contracting and expanding again—like your breath and your heartbeat do. These are the rhythms of life. If you experience hypoarousal, or the freeze response, you can learn, as Levine and Phillips (2012) say, "to go indirectly to the edges of where you are stuck," and "begin to move through and out of freeze and immobility" (69) where you have access to your action systems, the more active defenses of fight flight. This practice is powerful. It's called pendulation, a term coined by Levine. Some survivors worry they will always freeze up if they encounter any traumatic situations in the future. Through practicing pendulation, rather than reverting back to an immobilized trauma response (when unnecessary), you'll strengthen your capacity to mobilize when and if needed in the future. The following practice will introduce you to pendulation.

PRACTICE: Observing the Rhythms

For this practice, find a quiet place and try to make yourself as comfortable as possible, either seated or lying down. Stop if you feel overwhelmed or fearful.

- Close or softly focus your eyes. Take several slow, deep yet gentle breaths. Try to continue breathing this way throughout the exercise.

- Tune in to the sensations your body is experiencing now. See if you can become aware of both comfortable and uncomfortable sensations.

- Take some time to observe all you can about each sensation. For instance, is it uncomfortable, tight, jagged, hard, or comfortable, open, warm, energized?

- Allow your focus to stay with a comfortable sensation for a time, exploring its nuances. Where does the sense of comfort begin? Can you notice a shape and locate its edges? Does it change shape?

- Now, shift your focus to where an uncomfortable sensation is located; take your time to explore its subtle changes. If there's too much discomfort, shift back to the comfortable sensation or take a break and think of your positive resource.

- Continue to shift back and forth or pendulate at your own rhythm between the comfortable sensation and the uncomfortable sensation. Notice if you need to slow down your rhythm or speed it up and how each sensation changes or transforms.

- When you're ready, gently bring your attention back to your surroundings.

Take some time now to describe your experience. What sensations were present? Did they get smaller, larger, or shift in any way? Did you forget about the uncomfortable sensation when you focused on the comfortable sensation and vice versa?

_____

_____

_____

_____

_____

_____

You can also try this exercise with your resource from the "Object of Safety" practice, slowly shifting your focus back and forth from an internal sensation to your external resource. By learning to observe and track your sensations as they change, without becoming overstimulated, emotional pain will begin to feel manageable, and you'll no longer be stuck in habitual patterning. As you develop an embodied confidence that sensations are impermanent, rather than fearing them, triggering or distressing sensations, thoughts, and images will begin to lessen and shift altogether.

PRACTICE: Shape, Edges, Soften, Expand (SESE)

While it can be beneficial to stay with and observe a sensation, there are times you may want to generate movement with a sensation that feels stuck or uncomfortable.

- Begin by taking a few deep breaths as you ground and center yourself. Scan your body and notice any sensations calling your attention. If there are several, choose the loudest one to focus on. Try to release any stories or judgment about the discomfort and simply bring awareness to what is.

- Sense in and find the _shape_ of it. Where does it begin, and where does it end?

- Find the *edges* of the sensation, the outline of the shape or its border. You might also think of the edges as where comfort turns to discomfort. Where do you feel the sensation, and where does it feel neutral or even pleasant?

- Visualize or feel the edges and invite them to *soften.*

- If it feels comforting, gently place one or both hands in the area of the sensation and direct your breath there by visualizing your inhalation permeating the sensation.

- As you stay with the sensation, notice any subtle shifts. It may move, contracting and expanding or changing shape, or it may relax, and another sensation may call your attention.

- If it contracts and expands or changes shape, stay with it. If another sensation calls your attention loudly, do the above steps with the new sensation.

- After softening around it, offer the sensation more space by inviting it to *expand.* Let it move down into your arms, hands, and fingers, and down your legs to your feet.

- While you may fear giving the sensation more space, thinking it will strengthen the discomfort, in fact doing so helps it dissipate, usually lessening the intensity or relaxing the discomfort all together. Although it can seem counterintuitive, offering space works because it invites constricted muscles to relax.

- Notice if there's been any movement or shift. Stay with it as long as you'd like. Then gently bring your awareness back to your external environment.

Take a few minutes to reflect on your experience and write down what arose.

_____

_____

_____

_____

Orienting Your Attention

We all turn our attention toward selective environmental cues at the exclusion of others, especially those that are new or unfamiliar, in an attempt to determine whether they are safe or not safe. As you learned in chapter 1, survivors often unwittingly orient toward cues that serve as reminders of past trauma, things that appear to confirm negative thoughts and fears. There are many costs to inaccurately assessing safety, such as feeling unsupported or even threatened by people who love you and mean no harm or failing to assess danger accurately and finding yourself in threatening situations.

It's important to orient toward people and things that make you feel good and keep you safe, but with trauma, your evaluation of safe and not safe may have become skewed. One of my mentors, Bill Bowen, used to tell a story of a woman who attended one of his trainings, and then suddenly dropped out. She returned years later explaining that she'd left because she inexplicably didn't like him; in fact, she couldn't stand to look at him. As she'd progressed in her healing from trauma, she realized that she'd been orienting to his lips. Their shape resembled the lips of the man who'd molested her, and they were unconsciously and instinctively signaling not safe. Once she was able to recognize this and orient somewhere other than his lips, such as his eyes, she freed herself to learn from his vast knowledge, an opportunity that would have been lost had she continued to filter her orienting through trauma.

Another example is a young survivor I was working with who arrived at my office with her shoulders slumped forward and her head tilted downward in dorsal vagal collapse. Her vibrant energy had been replaced with fear and despair as she shared how triggering it had been to walk down the crowded city sidewalks on her way in. She tearfully shared that every man she passed served as a reminder of the abuser she'd escaped, leading her to feel confused, overwhelmed, and threatened as she questioned if each was capable of rape. What a horrifying thought, one that understandably and frequently threw her autonomic nervous system into immobilization. I reminded her that statistics show the majority of men are not rapists, that some of those men may also have been survivors, and suggested she look away from the men and orient toward women who appeared friendly or toward the buildings' architecture and other design elements. She chose to orient toward design and arrived in a calm state the following week ready to continue the work of healing.

By bringing awareness to the options available in each moment, you can begin to override involuntary instincts that rivet you to past triggers, allowing where you focus your attention to become more of a conscious choice. As a survivor, you always want to look for choice, because it was the lack of choice at the time of the assault(s) that resulted in your having become a victim. The next practice will help you cultivate choice in what you're orienting toward.

PRACTICE: What Are You Orienting Toward?

As you go about your day, notice what's drawing your attention and what's receding.

What do you orient toward when you wake up? Are you startled awake by the sound of an alarm, your roommate or partner, your child's cry or voice, your cat purring or dog licking you, sounds inside of your home, or sounds outside of your home? How does it feel to wake up to these sounds or anything else you orient toward?

_____

_____

_____

What else do you orient toward as you start your day?

_____

_____

_____

When you come into contact with another, where does your attention go? Is it to their eyes, mouth, nose, hair; the top of their head; their full face, or do you avoid looking at them?

_____

_____

_____

When you walk down a hallway or sidewalk, do you tend to look straight ahead, from side to side, down at the ground, or up?

_____

_____

_____

When you walk past people, do you tend to look for cues of safety or danger? For example, does your attention go to faces that appear happy, faces that are frowning, or faces that look aggressive?

_____

_____

_____

When you see someone from a distance walking toward you, what do you notice? From a distance, we're already evaluating safe–not safe. Notice how you do this. For example, is it based on their behavior, movements, posture, appearance?

_____

_____

_____

Do you tend to orient toward nature? If so, what draws your attention?

_____

_____

_____

Are there certain types of animals you orient toward? If so, why?

_____

_____

_____

What sounds do you orient toward? What draws you to them, such as high, low pitch, rhythmic?

_____

_____

_____

What objects do you orient toward? What elements of these objects attract you, such as color, shape, texture?

_____

_____

_____

Are there certain things people say that you tend to orient toward, such as positive feedback or criticisms?

_____

_____

_____

When you wind down your day, what do you orient toward before going to bed?

_____

_____

_____

You can answer the next questions at the end of the day or the following day.

Take some time to think about whether there were things on your list that made you feel unsafe. Notice what sensations you feel in your body as you think of these things. List the things that made you feel unsafe and their accompanying sensations.

_____

_____

_____

_____

Notice which things on your list contributed to positive feelings. As you connect with and list these things, describe what sensations are present in your body.

_____

_____

_____

_____

Were there any things on your list that made you feel safe? How do you recognize this in your body? Write down the sensations.

_____

_____

_____

_____

Is there anything you would like to orient more or less to? If so, can you think of ways you might do this and how it might feel in your body?

_____

_____

_____

_____

_____

_____

Orienting Your Awareness Log

When you orient toward certain people, situations, and things that cause discomfort, everything else that's going on around you is filtered out. Assuming there's no real present threat, it's important to listen to your body's cues for what makes you feel safe, calm, and comfortable. Then redirect your focus to those people, situations, and things. By choosing to catch and refocus what you're orienting toward, you'll free up your attention to receive all the little moments of nourishment and support you may have been missing.

As you bring awareness to what you naturally orient toward and begin to make choices about where you direct your attention, it can be helpful to keep a tracking log. Download the worksheet at http://newharbinger.com/46509.

You're doing a great job exploring new ground! If you begin to feel overstimulated orienting toward something new, remember to draw on pendulation from the "Observing the Rhythms" practice by bringing your focus back to a resource or place of comfort in your body. This will help you assess what you're experiencing with less reactivity.

In the next chapter, we'll look at how memory is impacted by trauma, identify your triggers, and learn strategies to help you cope.

CHAPTER 4

Trauma Memories and Triggers

Memory—data and information encoded, stored, and retrieved—is the way past events affect future function. An event becomes a trauma when overwhelming emotions interfere with memory processing. In *Sensorimotor Psychotherapy*, Ogden and Fisher (2015) write, "Whether we consciously remember the details of what happened, partially remember, or implicitly remember, our past experience has shaped who we are in the present" (479).

Even without trauma, memories are tricky in and of themselves. We remember selectively, and the more we recount a memory, the more it may develop a life of its own far removed from the original occurrence. You've probably noticed that the way you remember an experience can at times be drastically different from the way a friend or sibling recounts the same experience. This is in part due to your perspective, the lens you view the world from, but also because your memories are shifting and dynamically changing over time. Still, even with these shifts, your memories, both good and bad, create a cohesive narrative, a reasonably factual story with a beginning, middle, and end.

Traumatic memories differ from other memories in that they're fixed imprints, like a scar leaving deep marks or wounding on your body, brain, and psyche. Lacking a cohesive narrative, like a movie in your mind, trauma memories are said to be like shards of broken glass, fragmented splinters of undeveloped and unprocessed sensations, images, smells, tastes, emotions, and thoughts. The fragments are enough for your body to respond as if you were frozen in time experiencing the traumatic incident again and again. I've worked with survivors who've initially requested I turn off a fan, tuck a ticking clock into a drawer, or hide a teddy bear out of view because they couldn't yet tolerate these sounds or images. Their memories were intrusive, unintegrated fragments of traumas that hijack their nervous systems, causing the person to want to flee, want to curl into a ball, or to react by trembling or dissociating.

How a traumatic event is remembered varies from person to person. You may not remember or only partially remember what happened. You might do your best to avoid any traumatic memories and accompanying sensations, expending lots of energy to keep your emotions at bay. Perhaps you remember intellectually but feel distant from the event, unable to connect with the accompanying emotions and sensations, or you may be extremely eager to recount, make sense of, and process the fragmented images, sensations, and emotions disrupting your life.

Do you tend to avoid the memories and accompanying feelings and sensations, do you read and try everything you can get your hands on to put this behind you as quickly as possible, or is there some other way you relate to the traumatic incident?

_____

_____

Do you have a hard time feeling at all, or do you tend to feel too much in response to memories?

_____

_____

Neither avoiding nor reliving the memories supports healing. Avoiding keeps you stuck, while reliving the episode can reinforce the trauma. To facilitate integration of trauma, you can gradually awaken your awareness of related bodily sensations and emotions without having to recount in great detail the whole episode. It's essential that you and anyone working with you move at a slow enough pace to support the reorganization of the nervous system and formation of new patterns of sensation, actions, thoughts, and memories. This can be hard to hear if you want to rush the process, but going slow will pay off.

Memory Systems

Understanding how memory works has proven to be very helpful, and even a relief, for many of the survivors I've worked with. Memory can be divided into two main categories: explicit and implicit

Explicit memories are conscious recollections of factual information, concepts, and experiences. They are easily accessible, and you draw on explicit memory throughout the day when you remember things like the time of an appointment, a grocery list, or an event from years ago. An internal sense of remembering accompanies explicit memory recall.

Implicit memories are nonverbal and a combination of sensations, emotions, and behaviors that can't be accessed deliberately. They usually appear and disappear far outside of your conscious awareness. Implicit memories are formed in childhood, some in infancy before you acquired language. They're also formed in the wake of trauma; they are the dissociated memories that continue to strongly affect or trigger you—even on an unconscious level.

Explicit and implicit memories each have two broad subcategories.

Memory Systems

Explicit   Implicit

Semantic   *Episodic*   *Emotional*   *Procedural*

The first type of explicit memories are *semantic memories*, also known as *declarative memories*, and include facts, ideas, meaning, and concepts. They're objective, devoid of feeling, and independent of personal experience. An example of semantic memory is recalling what something is, such as a scooter, skateboard, or bicycle.

During a traumatic experience, information located in different parts of the brain, for example words, sounds, and images, can be prevented from combining to make a semantic memory. As discussed in chapter 2, when your nervous system goes into the sympathetic fight-flight response in an attempt to help you survive, your blood rushes away from your prefrontal cortex, the rational thinking part of your brain. This is one of the reasons why you probably don't have a clear memory of everything that happened during the traumatic experience.

The other type of explicit memories are *episodic memories* and are the autobiographical memories of an event or experience that are recalled or relived in detail. They form an interface between the explicit and implicit, promoting the formation of coherent narratives—the stories that help you make sense of your life. An example of an episodic memory is remembering where you were and who witnessed you when you fell from your scooter.

When a traumatic event occurs, episodic memory is shut down, and the sequence of events is fragmented. This, along with the dorsal vagal freeze response (discussed further in chapter 5), is another reason why you probably don't have a clear memory that plays like a movie from beginning to end of the trauma, instead remembering only certain fragments or moments.

Emotional memories, which are implicit, are the recollection of what you felt during an event experienced in your body as physical sensations. They encode important experiences for immediate reference in the future. Emotions signal what you might be needing or how best to respond in both social and survival situations. An example of an emotional memory is recalling the feeling of embarrassment after you fell off the scooter. After trauma, you may get triggered frequently, experiencing painful emotions that seem to come out of nowhere.

The other type of implicit memories are *procedural memories*, which are unconscious impulses, sensations, and movements, such as how to perform a task without actively thinking about it or what you're attracted to and what you're repulsed by. Procedural memories can be divided into three broad categories: learned motor actions, emergency responses, and tendencies to approach or avoid the things you feel attracted to or repulsed by (Levine 2015). An example of procedural memory is knowing how to get back on and ride the scooter after the fall without having to recall how to balance, propel, steer, or stop the scooter.

When you repeat a gesture, posture, or movement over and over again, it becomes habitual and automatic. Your procedural memory is recorded in these habitual patterns and speaks to you through the language of the body (Ogden and Fisher 2015). Unintegrated trauma can change your body's patterns of procedural memory. For instance, your body might begin to constrict and tense up in your stomach or pelvis, over time causing pain or making you more prone to injury. Or you might feel repulsed by and want to pull away from people or situations you didn't feel repulsed by before the trauma.

Traumatic memories are predominately emotional and procedural. This is why triggers and flashbacks are so disruptive—they're fragments of implicit procedural memories seemingly coming out of nowhere hijacking your nervous system into responding as though you're reliving the overwhelming event. Trauma disrupts the flow of information between these four memory subsystems (Levine 2015), which in turn disrupts your life. Healing brings them and you back into balance.

You Don't Have to Remember

It's not necessary to remember in order to heal. Survivors who've experienced only implicit memories are especially vulnerable to feeling like they need to have answers. Sadly, some are tormented by not knowing the truth of what happened. I understand. I had an implicit memory surface prior to my more obvious suppressed trauma memories. I'd been to a session with an energy and body worker the day before and left feeling kind of numb. The next day I was suddenly overtaken by intense pelvic floor pain and passed out. A short time later, I came to on my floor as a memory surfaced.

The visual was from the perspective of an infant in a crib. I saw the silhouette of a relative I'd feared as a child walk into the dark room. I heard their name. That was it. Curled up on the floor, I was overcome with terror, so much so that I couldn't get up. I crawled into the next room and remained on the floor confused and sobbing for what must have been an hour. In the following months, I longed to know the truth of what happened. I went to a therapist certified in hypnosis and regression therapy only to relive the same memory again, minus the intense physical pain and fainting.

I'll never know for certain what happened to me as an infant, but what I learned is that I don't need to know. Whether I'd picked up on it energetically (babies are good at that) or was in fact molested, it's clear I'd physically and emotionally felt intense fear about things a baby knows nothing about, and that's enough to tell me that something was off in that long-ago interaction and it needed to be healed. I invite you to explore your relationship to knowing and not knowing.

What happens inside you and what emotions and sensations are present when you think about knowing what happened?

_____

_____

What happens inside you when you think about not knowing? Write down the emotions and sensations.

_____

_____

Now imagine a place in-between, a place that makes room for both knowing and not knowing, a place that allows you the space to not have to decide for now. What does that feel like in your body?

_____

_____

It's understandable to want to know, but what needs prioritizing is your healing. If you're overwhelmed by surfacing memories, I recommend you work with a trauma-informed therapist, preferably one who's somatically trained. The therapist can help you touch into the memory one piece at a time without becoming further traumatized, while introducing new empowered bodily experiences, like those in this book. Once you're able to recall a traumatic memory from a resourced and empowered stance, your memory will be updated to include these implicit emotional and procedural memories without the nervous system activation.

Dual Awareness

Pat Ogden, creator of sensorimotor psychotherapy, teaches the importance of duel awareness as the antidote to two things: avoidance and preoccupation. Avoidance is distancing yourself from the body sensations that are actually needed to heal. Preoccupation is reliving the painful traumatic memories over and over again.

Avoidance prevents or inhibits healing because integrating the impact trauma has on your memory calls for activation of the same parts of your brain and body that were activated during the traumatic experience. The key to moving past distancing and reliving painful memories is to maintain awareness of your surroundings in the present moment (using the mindfulness techniques I shared in chapter 2) every time you remember or talk about the trauma. It's important to apply this practice whether you're thinking, talking, or implicitly remembering what happened. As you practice becoming more and more aware of how the memories affect your internal state, you'll begin to successfully process and integrate them.

You don't need to, nor do I want you to, relive the trauma. At the same time, as Ogden and Fisher (2015) write, "To integrate the effects of the memory, we must activate the same parts of the brain and body that were activated during the event, which means reexperiencing, to some degree, the state we were in when the event occurred" (479). "To some degree" is important here. Each time a memory surfaces or you're triggered, there's no need to try to remember more or force yourself to recount the whole episode. Instead, notice where you're placing your focus—your senses, emotions, thoughts, sensations, or movements—then choose to place your focus on one of the nondominant categories. Practicing this while continuing to maintain awareness in the present moment is a form of duel awareness. The next practice offers a specific way to do this when you experience an explicit or implicit memory. A downloadable copy is available at http://newharbinger.com/46509.

PRACTICE: Mindfully Remembering

Chose a recent explicit or implicit memory to work with. If you feel overwhelmed or activated any time, do "Coming into Safety" (chapter 1) and return to your resource as needed (chapter 3).

Ground and center yourself; then bring awareness to the present and your surroundings. What do you see, hear, smell, taste, and feel on your skin?

_____

_____

_____

_____

_____

Recalling the memory, which of your five senses were engaged?

_____

_____

Were you aware of any sensations?

_____

_____

Did your body move or have the impulse to move, even ever so slightly?

_____

_____

Can you name what emotions were present?

_____

_____

What thoughts arose?

_____

_____

Which of the above categories of memories stood out most to you?

_____

_____

Have the memories shown up in the same or a similar way in the past? If so, when?

_____

_____

If you answered yes to the last question, this is a pattern for you. Whether a pattern or not, the next time a memory surfaces, try focusing on one of the other categories away from the dominate one to help regulate your nervous system's arousal. For instance, if your sensations feel overwhelming, place your attention on one of your five senses, such as noticing and isolating each sound you hear in your environment. If traumatic images are showing up, try directing your awareness to naming what emotions are present. And if you're experiencing overwhelming thoughts, try focusing on your sensations. Be sure to pick a category that's not dominant. *Remember to practice mindfully placing your awareness on the present and shifting your focus to a less dominant category of perception whenever trauma memories surface.*

To Tell, Confront, Report—or Not?

As trauma begins to thaw and new fragments of memory come into awareness, the question of who to tell or whether to come out to a larger group often arises. If you haven't already, you may have a desire to speak your truth, to explain the struggles you've been going through and the ways the trauma has impacted you. If you previously disclosed, you may be unhappy with the responses you received. Perhaps you feel more resourced now and ready to try again in an attempt at a better outcome.

First and foremost, telling your story should always be your choice, ideally when you feel emotionally ready and safe doing so. No one should pressure you to tell, and while we will look at some of the reasons why you might want to, it's important you don't override your inner knowing, rushing or being pressured into telling your story before you're ready. It's okay to wait.

If you haven't told anyone, or told but didn't receive support, you may be afraid to talk about what you've been through. Perhaps you were taught that it's not okay to share, you can't be emotional, you shouldn't rock the boat, or you should just get over it or tough it out. The problem with these views is that they're isolating, leaving you alone with your pain and preventing you from finding supportive allies that aid in your healing. Healing requires you to vulnerably share your feelings and pain with another. Just one supportive ally can make you feel seen and help you begin to trust again.

Many survivors don't tell to protect others, family members, friends, families of the abuser, and even the abusers themselves. It's likely some people will be negatively impacted, but the perpetrator is the one responsible for any harm done to others as a result of their actions. If you're waiting to tell until no one will be uncomfortable or hurt by the truth, you'll never get to tell. If there's someone you want to tell whom you're protecting, carefully consider if this is what's best for you and your well-being. An example of this dilemma follows in the upcoming story about Chandra.

Incest and sexual assault take place under a veil of secrecy, which serves to shame the victim and protect the perpetrator. When I was assaulted as a teen, I held onto so much shame, thinking that mine was an isolated case, that what they did was a reflection of my unworthiness. I didn't tell for years. I was afraid to identify or be identified as a victim, so I subconsciously buried it instead. The problem is that you can't really bury it. Eventually it will surface, having taken even more of a physical and emotional toll. Breaking the secrecy is a powerful part of healing and reducing shame, isolation, and feelings of low self-worth.

Choice is a part of this process and can help create a feeling of safety. For instance, choosing the time of day, the setting, if an ally accompanies you, and what kind of support you want to request are all ways that you can have some control. There's also choice in how you tell. Sometimes writing a letter or email works best. I had one client who wrote a letter and then read it to family members individually, some in person and some over the phone. This helped her maintain boundaries and stay calmer than she would have if she'd had to recount the event over and over again. Another client wrote and sent an email to inform her former college faculty and cohort what she had been through while a student. Both of these young women focused on healing from symptoms first, then thoughtfully contemplated what they wanted to communicate, and had allies available to support them if needed. As a result, they maintained a level of control and were met with overwhelming support.

Of course, you can't control the responses you'll get when you share, so it's important to get clear on your expectations. Are they realistic or wishful thinking? Consider if the person you want to tell is somehow invested in your story not being true or in the truth not seeing the light of day. Any judgment, defensiveness, or inappropriate responses they have are about them. If they blame or shame you in any way, it's a reflection of them, not you. Bring in the "Self-Compassion Steps" from chapter 2 and reach out to an ally for support. If you don't have an ally and need support, you can call the RAINN twenty-four-hour hotline: 1-800-656-4673.

As you break the silence that has constrained you, speaking your truth and correcting any false or inaccurate information, you'll gain ownership over your narrative, which in turn fosters healing.

Reporting

If you're deciding whether to do a rape kit (a forensic exam conducted soon after an assault), report, or move forward with a case, it's important to know some facts. If you decide to have an exam to collect DNA, you have the right to stop, pause, or skip a step at any point during the exam. With the exception of minors, once the evidence is collected, you can choose to report the assault then, at a later time, or not at all. You can read more about what to expect during the exam at https://www.rainn.org/articles/rape-kit. Reporting, especially within seventy-two hours of the assault, will increase the likelihood of identifying and prosecuting the perpetrator, which can prevent future sexual assaults from occurring.

Unfortunately, only five out of every one thousand rapists are convicted in the US. It's a very discouraging number to say the least. The man who assaulted Chanel Miller is one of the 0.5 percent. Her victim-impact statement (available online) and best-selling book, *Know My Name*, paint a vivid picture of her challenging ordeal navigating the legal system, ultimately speaking her truth and reclaiming her name. Miller's high-profile case helped to expedite DNA evidence, but most states have an overwhelming backlog on testing rape kits, and lack of DNA evidence is one of the biggest obstacles to prosecuting perpetrators. There are several programs and initiatives working to address this issue, although progress is slow.

Much of our legal system is based on assumptions about what the victim should or shouldn't have done. Unfortunately, many police officers, lawyers, judges, and medical professionals don't have the necessary understanding of what happens to the brain and body during and after trauma. This lack of training and, at times, lack of compassion can lead victims to be further traumatized and to mirror negative societal responses by shaming or blaming themselves. If you sought help or reported, you may have felt retraumatized and burdened with yet another aspect of the traumatic wound to heal from. Miller (2019) wrote of her legal ordeal, "When society questions a victim's reluctance to report, I will be here to remind you that you ask us to sacrifice our sanity to fight outdated structures that were designed to keep us down" (288).

Like the majority of survivors, you may not have reported. Perhaps you were underage and didn't know how to put into words what happened to you, or it may not have been safe for you to report. Overwhelming feelings of shock, fear, and shame may have immobilized you. You may have intentionally chosen to protect someone or to spare putting yourself through the ordeal. These are all valid reasons. You did what you could or had to do to survive in the aftermath of the assault.

How do you feel about having reported or not reported?

_____

_____

_____

If the statutes of limitation for reporting have not run out in your state, you may still have the option. Are there any legal actions you want to take now or eventually, once you're ready?

_____

_____

_____

Remember, you did the best you could with the internal and external resources you had at the time. If any feelings of shame or regret are present, bring in the "Self-Compassion Steps" and remind yourself that you made the best choice you could under the circumstances you were in. If anger is alive within you, give it some healthy expression—journal, draw, or paint it; vocalize it; or physicalize it by sensing into how your body wants to move. We'll explore working with anger, shame, and other emotions in chapter 7.

— Story: Chandra

Chandra was attending a work conference in another city when she met two female friends in the hotel bar. Two men seated at a nearby table sent over a bottle of wine then joined the three of them. Chandra had two glasses, the only drinks she consumed that night. She woke up several hours later in a stranger's room having been drugged and sexually assaulted. She went to the hospital and reported the assault only to be further traumatized by the rape kit process, particularly the inappropriate and uncompassionate comments of a nurse. Her assailant, who resided in another country was identified, but Chandra decided it was best for her health to not put herself through the long, arduous, expensive, and potentially further traumatizing court process in an attempt to gain some form of justice.

It had been about a year since the incident when Chandra came to see me. She was struggling with frequent triggers and difficulty making boundaries. After the assault, she'd reached out to the friends who'd joined her that evening, and to her dismay, she was met with minimal support or empathy, which felt further wounding. Given the nurse and her friends' responses, Chandra was fearful of opening up to anyone else, yet she yearned for understanding, compassion, and support from those closest to her, especially her mother.

As part of her treatment, we worked through intense feelings of the misdirected shame I described in the last section, so common among survivors, until she felt able to reach out to her mother for support. Soon after, her mother came to visit, giving her the opportunity to open up about the trauma and resulting symptoms. This proved to be healing for Chandra as she finally began to receive the support she'd longed for.

A few weeks later, Chandra learned she had to go back to the same city for the same conference, and to make matters worse, the company was putting her up in the same hotel. She was terrified of returning to the location of the assault and terrified of being triggered in front of her colleagues who had no idea what she was going through. Her mother offered to fly out and stay with her during the conference, but Chandra was concerned how it would look to her colleagues.

We discussed how her mother's companionship would be a healthy way to help regulate her nervous system and ease the potential triggers of being back in the same hotel. We also looked at what type of boundaries she might make with her colleagues regarding disclosure of her mother's presence. Chandra decided to take her mother up on her offer. Her mother was there for her during the times she feared most, before and after conference meetings, and proved to be a supportive ally. She even spoke to hotel security on Chandra's behalf, providing them with the name and description of her assailant, so they could be warned if he returned and possibly prevent him from assaulting another.

— *Story:* Sophie

Like Chandra, Sophie longed for the support of her mother but was not ready to tell her. As a teen, Sophie was molested by her stepfather. Several years later, she confided in a close relative and a few friends. Each responded firmly that she could not tell her mother, who had recently recovered from an addiction. They feared her mother would relapse if she learned the truth. Telling her could also lead to her choosing to end her marriage. Although intellectually Sophie knew that it was her stepfather's actions, not her own, that would be responsible for any fallout, she didn't want to carry the burden of revealing the truth.

Sophie and I explored and processed her feelings of internalized shame. Shame can limit one's sense of choice, and as previously mentioned, it's when choice is taken away from us that we become victims. In Sophie's case, it was empowering to realize she does in fact have choice. It's no one else's place to tell her who she can or can't speak her truth to. For now, she chooses to withhold what happened, knowing that at any point, she can decide differently. Even if she never feels it's the right time to confide in her mother, she's gained tremendous agency in acknowledging that the choice belongs to her.

These two stories illustrate that there's no one right answer to when and who you should tell. It's your decision. What matters is that your decision feels like it's best for you now, and in the long run.

To help you assess what you do and don't want to do, download the "Questions to Consider Before Telling Others" worksheet at http://newharbinger.com/46509.

Triggers Are Images and Feelings from the Past That Need Healing

Triggers happen in a flash as automatic responses connected to past trauma—pieces of sensory, emotional, or somatic memories that suddenly disrupt the present. They act like cracks in present-day reality that open to unresolved trauma from the past. In *Healing Sex,* Staci Haines (1999) writes, "Triggers are history seeping through into the present, pieces of memory emerging from the past. While the pain, anger, or confusion can seem to be a response to something that is happening today, [a trigger] is really a fragment of visual, emotional, or body memory making its way to the surface" (249).

Triggers can be anything your mind perceives as similar to the traumatic event: a sound, a tone of voice, a word, a name, painful emotions often without context, thoughts about the past or a similar situation, a topic of conversation, media and films, the temperature, the environment, smells, touch, facial characteristics, gestures, a posture, a movement, a person, a color, an object, a place, and more. We get triggered by good memories as well, associating a song with a memory of someone we love and a happy time in our life or the smell and taste of a particular food with comfort.

Unlike flashbacks, with trauma triggers, you know where you are and what time it is. When triggered, you automatically neurocept these pieces of memory from the past as threatening even though they're not, instinctively listening to bodily signals that tell you you're in danger. They can bring on tears, fear, anger, or shame and cause you to tremble, feel short of breath, nauseous, act out, or withdraw. Given how disruptive and painful they can be, it's not uncommon for trauma survivors to organize their life in an attempt to minimize or avoid triggers altogether.

Are there any triggers that you go out of your way to avoid?

_____

_____

_____

It's okay to avoid triggers while healing. The problem with this in long run is that your life will become more and more restricted and isolating. Rather than making your world smaller, ultimately you want to get to a place of no longer being triggered by the traumatic event.

Triggers point you in the direction of what needs healing. As you become aware of the sensations and bodily movements that signal a trigger, you'll have the opportunity to learn to calm your nervous system, and then to process the material and begin to move through it. I find EMDR especially helpful with stubborn triggers. If you have the means, you might seek out an EMDRIA-certified therapist specializing in trauma, but there are many other ways to work with triggers. The first step is to become aware of your triggers as they're happening, next you can look at strategies to help you diffuse your triggers, and finally it helps map your triggers. Mapping supports you in identifying what brings them on, noticing what self-soothing strategies work best for you, and recognizing the healing taking place as your triggers decrease in frequency and duration. We'll start with looking at self-soothing and defusing strategies.

Defusing Your Triggers

Choose some options from the following list, which is available for download at http://newharbinger. com/46509, to have on hand when triggered. Which ones resonate with you? Check off any that you want to try.

☐ Remind yourself of the year and the date; you are here in the present.

☐ Think of your external resource, hold it, look at it, or visualize it ("An Object or Image of Safety," chapter 3), or connect with your internal resource ("A Place of Strength or Calm," chapter 3).

☐ Pick an object in the room or environment, notice every detail as though you were going to paint it, and mindfully stay present with it.

☐ Focus on listening to the sounds in whatever environment you're in, alternate isolating one at a time, and then hearing the combined symphony of sound.

☐ Move around, stretch, and shake or brush off the trigger.

☐ Try changing your posture. For example, if your shoulders are collapsed, pull them up and back a bit. If they're tense, try relaxing them, sitting back in a chair, and taking some deep calming breaths.

☐ Wash your face with ice water, dip your hands in a bowl of ice, or hold an ice cube to the back of your neck.

☐ Mindfully sip a warm cup of tea or wrap yourself in a blanket. You might look into weighted blankets, which are known to help alleviate anxiety.

☐ Hug a pillow, stuffed animal, person you trust, or pet.

☐ Practice the "Self-Compassion Steps" (chapter 2).

☐ Reach out to a friend, ally, or loved one for support.

☐ If you have a dog, cat, or other furry friend, spend some time petting or brushing them. A cat's purr and a dog's loyalty are very healing.

☐ Talk to the triggered part of yourself. Ask what it wants to say and what it is needing. Is there anything you can do to meet this need in a healthy way?

☐ Treat the trigger as though it were your inner child, vulnerable and upset. How can you take care of and comfort this child?

☐ If you're at work, take a moment to tell the activated part of you that you want to hear why they got triggered, but you can't be present at this time. Let the part know that you'll spend time with them later and find time to do so after work.

☐ Get engaged in another activity, such as going for a walk or watching a movie, while staying aware of what you're experiencing (sensations, feelings, thoughts).

☐ Visualize a different and better outcome to any visual memory that may have been triggered. Get creative and bring in superhero abilities or a hero/heroine who protects you.

☐ Visualize sending the trigger out into space and watch as it gets smaller and smaller until it disappears.

☐ Journal or draw about your experience.

List any other trigger strategies that have been or might be helpful to you.

_____

_____

_____

_____

PRACTICE: Trigger Strategy

- First do your best to come into safety (chapter 1).

- Next take note of what's triggering you. Don't worry if you don't have an answer. It may come to you later. What's important is that you grow your awareness of when you've been triggered.

- Notice what emotion you're feeling, and be precise about labeling it. Is it fear, overwhelm, anger, shame? If, for example, it's fear, what type of fear is it: suspicious, worried, panic, dread? You'll find a list of challenging emotions at http://newharbinger.com/46509, which can help with this process.

- Then ask yourself if there's anything you're needing. This could be any number of things from the preceding list.

PRACTICE: Trigger Mapping and Tracking

It's helpful and even empowering to be able to identify your triggers. When you feel one coming on, you can remind yourself that it's your nervous system being activated by something that happened in the past, that it's uncomfortable, but it will pass. Think of which tools you can use in the moment, and give yourself permission to seek out more privacy, if needed. The more you understand your triggers, the better prepared you'll be to anticipate problems, understand what's happening, lessen their intensity, and calm yourself. This worksheet is also at http://newharbinger.com/46509.

Trigger mapping. I've divided triggers into seven categories: the five senses (hearing, sight, smell, taste, touch), sensations, and emotions. Take some time to identify and list any triggers you've experienced in each category. Add to your list as your awareness grows and enjoy crossing triggers off the list as you move forward in your healing.

Hearing (Examples: the tone of someone's voice, sirens, a ticking clock, the rain, a word.)
Sight (Examples: the expression on someone's face, a particular color, a building or city block.)
Smell (Examples: coffee brewing, a cologne, the scent of someone's perspiration, alcohol.)
Taste (Examples: something bitter, a particular food or beverage, the air before a storm.)
Touch (Examples: an unwanted hug, a part of your body, two little or two much pressure.)
Sensations (Examples: body memories, constricted throat, racing heart, upset stomach.)
Emotions (Examples: fear, terror, shame, vulnerability, anger, rage, hopeless, despair.)

Trigger tracking. The next time you're triggered, list the date and duration. Then describe the trigger, what it was preceded by, what sensations and emotions you felt, and what helped you calm down.

Date _____ Duration _____

I got triggered when: _____

Sensations I felt: _____

Emotions I felt: _____

What helped to calm me: _____

_____

Date _____ Duration _____

Trigger: _____

Sensations: _____

Emotions: _____

What helped: _____

_____

Date _____ Duration _____

Trigger: _____

Sensations: _____

Emotions: _____

What helped: _____

_____

Date _____ Duration _____

Trigger: _____

Sensations: _____

Emotions: _____

What helped: _____

_____

Date _____ Duration _____

Trigger: _____

Sensations: _____

Emotions: _____

What helped: _____

_____

Date _____ Duration _____

Trigger: _____

Sensations: _____

Emotions: _____

What helped: _____

_____

Date _____ Duration _____

Trigger: _____

Sensations: _____

Emotions: _____

What helped: _____

_____

Date _____ Duration _____

Trigger: _____

Sensations: _____

Emotions: _____

What helped: _____

_____

After you've tracked several triggers over a few weeks, come back to this exercise to answer the following questions.

Do you notice any patterns?

_____

_____

_____

_____

Are there any other steps you can take when triggered to regulate your nervous system and calm yourself?

_____

_____

_____

_____

Do you want to add or cross anything off your trigger map?

_____

_____

Have you noticed any change in frequency or duration?

_____

_____

We've covered a lot of ground, and you're doing good work! Healing takes time, so be kind and patient with yourself and don't forget your self-compassion practice.

CHAPTER 5

Making Sense of Dissociation, Flashbacks, and Fear

During and following a traumatic event you may shut down your emotions and capacity to connect with your body to distance yourself from the pain and terror that accompany trauma. You might become dazed, numb, or checked-out, or feel very small or like you're floating outside of your body. This is called dissociation, a physical and emotional state that accompanies the dorsal vagal freeze response. Essentially, your body's release of pain-reducing endorphins results in the numbing of physical sensations and an altered state of awareness. It can range from subtle, like spacing out, to extreme, as in the case of traumatic amnesia.

One client compared dissociation to looking through a camera lens, describing it as a feeling of being out of focus. As she gradually came into her body, the lens moved a little bit back into focus, and then fully came in focus when she felt calm and grounded.

Why We Dissociate

Dissociation occurs when you've been through a traumatic experience dangerous enough to be a threat to your well-being or life while in a state of relative helplessness. It's your body's way of getting you through the traumatic event, but dissociation can continue to surface years after the danger's over every time you're exposed to a trauma cue, pulling you back into that state of helplessness. It's a needed survival mechanism, yet left untreated, prevents the traumatic event from being fully resolved or healed.

As dissociation thaws, procedural memories (described in chapter 2) may increase. These memories include all the somatic information from the traumatic event stored as a means to enhance your future survival skills. When trauma isn't resolved, these memories can be considered unintegrated parts of yourself. Everyone has parts, such as the part that responds like a vulnerable child. You may have a spaced-out part, an obedient part, or a timid and mute part to name just a few. These parts are communicating what had been needed to help you survive the trauma. When they surface, you may remember disjointed pieces of the traumatic event, nothing at all, or have a full visual replay. It doesn't matter how much you remember; what matters most is that embodiment is the antidote to dissociation.

What Happens When You Dissociate?

Just like with triggers, the more you understand what happens to you when you dissociate, the better prepared you'll be for lessening the intensity and calming yourself as you find your way back. If relevant, consider what is it like when you dissociate.

Where do you go?

_____

_____

What are you thinking?

_____

_____

What do you say to yourself?

_____

_____

Do you notice what parts are present? Describe those parts.

_____

_____

How does the world look to you when you dissociate?

_____

_____

Now pay attention to what happens in your body. Is your breath shallow?

_____

Are you holding your breath?

_____

Can you feel your arms and legs?

_____

Do you feel any sensation in your back?

_____

Are you tensing the muscles in your jaw, shoulders, abdomen, pelvic floor, or anywhere else?

_____

_____

Are there places where your body feels frozen or numb? Write down where.

_____

_____

— Story: Monica

Monica had a traumatic childhood that included witnessing the violent death of one of her parents. Her first relationship in college appeared to be emotionally supportive, but, like so many women who find themselves in abusive relationships, Monica didn't see the signs of domestic violence until she was sexually assaulted. She got out of the relationship, but it took a tremendous emotional and physical toll. She was diagnosed with PTSD soon after she graduated.

I see this often: young women who were sexually assaulted in college and somehow manage to suppress the traumatic event long enough to graduate, only to see an increase in symptoms soon after. Of course, this isn't a conscious choice. You don't really have a say in when your brain will *suppress the trauma and when your body will scream for help with symptoms that demand your attention.*

Months into treating Monica, she called one day for support. She woke up feeling as though she were in a fog. Tearfully she shared that she felt like a victim, dissociated. I walked her through "Coming into Safety" (CIS). This generated enough change to help her nervous system move in the direction of ventral vagal calm, but she still felt numb. I asked, "What parts of yourself can you feel?" Monica slowly scanned her body and answered, "My shoulders, face, eyes, hand, and heart" (her hands were still resting over her heart).

I directed Monica to gently place her hands on her numb abdomen and to ask her body what was needed. I explained that an answer might come in the form of an image, word, or phrase. Monica said, "They're far away," "they" being her dissociated parts. I suggested she tell them, "It's safe to come back now." Monica's tears returned as she told me she didn't know if it was safe. She declined doing CIS a second time, stating, "I don't need to." I responded, "When it's safe, place your hands on your abdomen, take your time, and when you're ready, tell your abdomen that you're safe." A moment later I heard, "I'm back."

I asked if there was another part of her that felt numb. Monica replied her legs. Again, I asked her to place her hands on her legs; she said it was hard. I reassured her the same steps would help her legs come back: to ask if there was anything needed, then to let them know it was safe, and invite them back. There was a pause. Then she said, "They're back, the tops of my legs, but my calves are numb." I suggested she situate herself so she could comfortably place her hands on her calves then do the same steps. She did, followed by her feet, and finally her arms.

Monica explained, "It's strange. It feels like after you've run. I feel very alive." She was right. When you come back into yourself, you're free to experience all of the flavor and fullness of being alive. This is why embodiment is the antidote to dissociation. You too can invite yourself back into your body using the same process.

PRACTICE: Inviting Yourself Back

Awareness of your body's unique signals preceding dissociation is half the battle. Be mindful of what sensations, feelings, and thoughts show up (as you did in the "What Happens When You Dissociate?" section) when you're on your way out. The next time you dissociate, the sooner you try the following suggestions, the sooner you'll come back into your body.

- Do "Coming into Safety," from chapter 1. If you're unable do all of the steps, even doing one or two steps can help.

- Place your hands on a numb area of your body, ask what is needed, and then invite it back as you let this part know that in this moment it's safe. Repeat this on any other areas that feel numb.

- If seated or lying, try standing up. This can increase a sense of safety.

- Imagine a string attached to the top of your head. Now imagine someone pulling it up as though you were a marionette. Lengthening your spine can counteract the parasympathetic hypoarousal immobilization and numbing.

- Raise your arms and hands in front of you as though you were telling someone to stop. This engages the boundary muscles of your abdomen, creating a sense of protection.

- Pick any of your chosen trigger strategies from chapter 4.

When you experience a flashback or dissociate, you're in a mild state of hypnotic trance, believing that you're reliving the past traumatic event. This trance state can be directed toward an imaginative inner safe place or protective figure (Fisher 2014). Create these resources when you're in a calm state so you have them ready to draw on the next time you find yourself immobilized. Use the "A Place of Strength or Calm" practice from chapter 3 to find your safe place. The next time you dissociate, imagine going to your safe place, and then slowly tap it in using the "Tapping in the Good" practice from chapter 3. Now respond to the following questions.

1. Write a description of your safe place.

_____

_____

_____

_____

2. Imagine a *protective figure*. This can be an imagined or real person, a combination of qualities from several people, an angel or guide, an animal, or a superhero. Imagine them fully, and then take note of their eyes, what they say to you, and how they comfort you. Again, when you feel connected, tap them in. If more than one shows up, tap each in. Write a description of your protector(s).

_____

_____

_____

_____

The next time you dissociate, bring up the image of your protector(s) and slowly tap them in.

3. Try noticing what part of you is present. Ask the part what they're needing now. Is there a safe place they want to go to or a protective figure they want to call on?

_____

_____

Experiment to learn what works best for you, the more you practice, the easier it will become. To help you become more aware of what causes you to check out and what helps bring you back, download the "Dissociative Experience Log" at http://newharbinger.com/46509.

Flashbacks

Flashbacks are jumbled fragments of memory being replayed and reexperienced as uninvited incoherent intrusions or physical symptoms. When experiencing a flashback, it feels as though you're reliving the traumatic event. The same stress hormones flow through your veins, and the same nervous system reactions are evoked, preparing your body to react as it did at the time of the initial trauma. Not all survivors experience flashbacks, but for those who do, they can wreak havoc on your life until resolved.

It's common to think of flashbacks as visual or auditory replays of the traumatic event, but they also appear in the form of intrusive bodily sensations, such as a feeling of being trapped, a sense of panic, or feeling helpless with no conscious memory responsible for stimulating these feelings. One of the ways flashbacks showed up during my healing journey were as bouts of vertigo.

The triggering event was viewing the 1965 black-and-white film *Cut Piece,* a performance by Yoko Ono in which members of the audience stepped up to the stage one by one to cut a small piece of fabric from her modest dress. While most were very respectful, one man was extremely aggressive, cutting away a large piece exposing her skin and bra. The expression on Yoko's face pained me. We were witnessing her being violated, yet in a discussion after the film, no one else seemed fazed by it. At home that night as I leaned back onto my pillow, I suddenly became extremely dizzy, followed by confusion and fear.

Flashbacks catch you off guard. These jumbled fragments of memory can cause you to feel terrified, out of control, or like you're losing it as they pull you back into the encapsulated past, leaving you out of touch with your current situation. The vertigo continued off and on for several months whenever I'd lay my head back (when practicing yoga, at the chiropractor's office, on my bed), leaving me feeling fearful, confused, and unable to trust my body. Eventually I realized the exact connection of the vertigo to the traumas: I'd been forced to *lie back* on a pillow during the assaults. Although I didn't yet have the language for it, the fear, confusion, and dizziness I'd been experiencing was due to the overwhelm of fragmented procedural body-based memories (as described in chapter 4).

Flashbacks pull your attention away from any safety and security in the present moment as you lose touch with your current situation. In *Trauma and Memory*, Peter Levine (2015) writes, "The more we try to rid ourselves of these 'flashbacks,' the more they haunt, torment, and strangle our life-force, seriously restricting our capacity to live in the here and now" (7). When you're able to process and assimilate these intrusions, coherent memories are formed, restoring continuity between past and future. Yet even though a fragment of memory has presented itself, when you're in the midst of a flashback, don't try to process or work through the traumatic memory. Instead, what's needed is to *contain the memory and to orient to the present moment* using any of the skills you have learned so far.

Another factor to keep in mind is how you're evaluating external reality. People typically use their external senses (exteroception) to scan and evaluate the environment for safety. As discussed in chapter 3, survivors can be fooled into thinking there's danger when there's not, or vice versa, due to disruption of internal and external sensory perception. This leads trauma survivors to routinely evaluate external reality based on what they feel inside (proprioception and interoception). *Evaluating external reality by inner sensations is how a flashback takes hold. You need to draw on both internal and external senses to be and feel genuinely safe.*

Keeping the Past in the Past

It's important to state to yourself that a flashback is not a replay or repetition of the trauma; it's a memory of the event. In *8 Keys to Safe Trauma Recovery*, Babette Rothschild (2010) explains that the simple recognition that a flashback is a memory has "the power to instantly reduce the intensity of, and even stop, a flashback in its tracks" (62). The next time you have a flashback, try reminding yourself, *This is a memory; the trauma is not happening now.* You can create a mantra specific to you, as long as you don't include intensifying details of your trauma. It may help to say the words out loud, to write them down, or record them on your phone.

Think of a sentence or phrase that will help remind you the trauma is in the past, such as, "Today is Monday, May 3, 2021. I'm okay; I survived," or "I'm an adult now. I'm no longer dependent. They can't hurt me anymore."

_____

_____

_____

To avoid intensifying the flashback, acknowledge that the trauma occurred in the past. Always use past-tense verbs when talking during or describing a flashback. Rothschild suggests changing a present-tense phrase, such as, "I feel him…!" to the past tense, such as, "When he….," or "When I was…" This will help lessen the activation taking place within your nervous system. It's okay to say, "I'm having a flashback," since the flashback itself is occurring in the present (Rothschild 2010). Download the "Flashback Strategies" handout at http://newharbinger.com/46509.

PRACTICE: The Container Exercise

Containment imagery is used in many therapy modalities, such as EMDR, to help aid in containing memories. The container isn't meant to be used to lock things away indefinitely. Rather it's used to contain an overwhelming memory until you can work with it at a later time when you're not as activated or with a trauma-informed therapist.

- Ground and make yourself comfortable.

- Imagine a container. It can be any size or shape and made of any material you wish. It can be beautiful and ornate or something simple like a paper box or a jar. The important thing is that it has a lid that closes tightly.

- Once you have a clear image of your container, try slowly tapping it in on one side of your body then the other seven or more times (as you did in "Tapping in the Good").

- If there's a challenging memory and accompanying feelings and sensations that you want to put in your container, open it up and imagine putting them inside one at a time.

- Slowly tap them in.

- Now close the container nice and tightly.

- Tap in.

- You can give the container a name if you wish.

- Tap it in.

Describe your container.

_____

_____

What did you experience?

_____

_____

Did you notice any shift after you tapped in the memory?

_____

_____

Flashbacks can be very powerful, so be kind and gentle with yourself. Give yourself time to recover as you appreciate and honor yourself for having survived.

Dreams and Nightmares

Dreams are a portal into your personal experiences of daily life, thoughts, images, and sensations that can help you meet your problems in a more creative, productive, and joyful way. A dream is an experience you have in a nonmaterial invisible realm of the soul, communicated in a language that differs from that of waking language. The events of the dream are usually symbolic, often depicting desires or fears. As you dream, you're viewing your life from a new angle, and in doing so, you may gain important insights.

For survivors, dreams can feel unsafe or even terrifying. They can show up in the form of recurrent nightmares or night terrors and include details of past trauma that disrupt sleep to the extent that sleep is avoided.

Do you ever find yourself avoiding sleep? If so, what do you do to put off sleep, and how do you feel about this?

_____

_____

Do you have recurrent nightmares? If so, have you noticed a theme?

_____

_____

Do you know about sleep hygiene—things like turning off all devices an hour or more before sleep, wearing special glasses or setting devices to filter out the blue light on your screens in the evening, not drinking caffeine past noon, and not eating sugar in the evening or cutting it out all together? These are just some of many things you can do to help with sleep. Is there anything you want to try?

_____

_____

Without adequate sleep, you're more likely to feel anxious, depressed, off your game, irritable, and not fully present, and this can negatively impact your long-term health. The origins of trauma nightmares lie in both the trauma you experienced and in your high arousal state. Working to lessen your nervous system's arousal and getting seven to nine hours of sleep a night will help. It can also help to talk or journal about the theme of the nightmare.

I had a recurrent nightmare for over a year in what I now realize was a foreshadowing of my sexual trauma surfacing. In the dream I would awaken to a male silhouette with a raised weapon in one hand standing over my bed. I'd wake up terrified, trembling, and screaming, but little or no sound would come out of my mouth. One night, soon after calling a hotline for support on a day that a disheveled man had tried to assault me in a parking lot, I had the nightmare again. Only this time, the dream figure was no longer in silhouette. As I recognized the familiar face of a relative, he was rendered powerless, and I never had the nightmare again. Reaching out for support through the hotline helped me process the attempted assault, which in turn facilitated the reveal of the dream metaphor. This speaks to the value in processing your dreams whether through keeping a dream journal or speaking to a trusted friend or therapist.

Waking Up in Fight, Flight, or Freeze

If you frequently wake up from unsettling dreams feeling fearful, depressed, or finding it hard to face the day, try setting two alarms—one for half an hour to forty-five minutes earlier. Then go back to sleep until the second alarm goes off at the time you need to wake up. I don't know for certain why this helps but speculate it's the completion of a disrupted REM cycle or not waking up in REM. REM sleep is characterized by the rapid eye movement it's named for, a faster pulse and breathing, and more dreaming and bodily movement. When you're asleep, REM and non-REM sleep alternate within one cycle that lasts about ninety minutes, with REM lengthening until you awake. One explanation for REM sleep suggests its purpose is to process procedural memories. I've found that going back to sleep helps with processing. I awake the second time feeling ready to face the day. Many of my clients have found this works for them as well.

Befriending Your Dreams

Processing nightmares can help you understand their meaning and metaphors, desensitizing you to their content, and reducing hyperarousal. Dreams often have more than one level of meaning and multiple messages. If you have the support of a therapist, share any traumatic dream content in session. If you don't, take it slow. If you get overly activated, stop and go back to your resources to generate movement toward calm and safety.

When first starting to treat patients on a reservation, psychologist Eduardo Duran noticed that people started getting well just by telling their dreams. He learned from the Indigenous people that everything has a spirit and to give offerings to your dream, as the dream is an entity also. In *Healing the Soul Wound,* Duran (2014) suggests giving the dream entity a gift and identify with it; know you're in relation with it. According to natural law, if you offer the dream entity a gift and ask what it wants, it has to respond. The answer will come in a dream or some other form of response, such as a message in your waking life.

Another form of ritual is to let go of the day before you go to sleep, knowing that everything will be there when you wake up. It can help to shake or brush off the day from your body with sweeping downward motions on your arms, torso, and legs. Next, set the intention to have peaceful dreams. If you connect with a guide, spirit animal, angle, or some other entity, you can ask them to watch over you, keeping you safe and calm while you dream. Give them gratitude when you awake.

Take a few minutes to imagine a dream ritual. Use any of the suggestions above and add whatever feels right to you, such as writing a mantra, calling in protectors, burning sage or incense, defusing essential oils, lighting a candle (be sure to blow it out before you fall asleep), or putting healing stones, stuffed animals, or other meaningful possessions near your bed. Let your imagination run wild; it's your creation.

_____

_____

_____

_____

Fear and Intuition: How to Distinguish Between the Two

Your body's an important source of intuition, providing a wellspring of wisdom to inform, protect, and inspire you. When you're able to balance intuition with logic, you have a much greater quantity of information to draw on. Albert Einstein reportedly said, "The intuitive mind is a sacred gift, and the rational mind is a faithful servant. We have created a society that honors the servant and has forgotten the gift." As a survivor, it's crucial to learn to listen to and honor the gift, your inner knowing. Those gut feelings, hunches, and flashes of insight can all be great allies in helping to keep you safe.

There are biological causes for intuitive experiences, that sense of knowing you sometimes have in your heart or gut is neurology at work. In *The Pocket Guide to Interpersonal Neurobiology*, Daniel J. Siegel (2012) defines intuition as "the nonlogical knowing that emerges from the processing of the body, especially the parallel distributed processors of the neural networks in the heart and intestines that send their signals upward, through the insula, to regions of the middle prefrontal cortex" (AI-43). The insula is a region of the brain deep in the cerebral cortex that receives input from interoceptive sensors, especially those located in your heart and gut. In simpler terms, Siegel (2012) says intuition is "having access to the input from the body and its nonrational ways of knowing that fuel wisdom" (27-3).

What gets in the way of intuition is fear, not valuing it, or extremely altered states from substances, such as alcohol. When I was assaulted while running, I hadn't yet fully understood the importance of trusting my intuition. If I had, I would've stayed home. Instead the pressure to get exercise outweighed the uncomfortable voice inside that lead me to ask others to join me on the run. When no one was available, I opted to go alone, as I often did and have hundreds of times since. As I ran up a slight incline in a suburban residential neighborhood, a man ran past me, and once again the uncomfortable feeling rose inside me. I thought of turning around and running in the opposite direction, but I was halfway up the block and headed home. I overrode my intuition a second time with reason, thinking, *He's ahead of me, so I must be safe,* but I was not. From then on, I learned to value my intuition. When I get that feeling, I skip the run, I'm more mindful of my surroundings, and I take a taxi or Lyft or do whatever I need to do to protect myself and honor my inner knowing.

Like me, you may have learned as a child to doubt your intuition. If so, you'll want to train your intellect to listen to, value, and express your intuitive voice. You can learn to cultivate and value intuition in the exercises that follow, and you can choose to avoid drinking and other substances in situations where you might be vulnerable, which brings us to fear. It can be challenging to differentiate a gut feeling from fear.

How We Orient Toward Fear

First, I want to acknowledge that the assault you suffered was one of, if not the worst, thing that's happened in your life. What I want you to explore here is the fear that doesn't correlate with a clear or obvious danger. This is the kind of fear that blocks access to your intuition.

How many times have you obsessively worried or feared something that never came to pass? It's natural to get caught in the grip of fear from time to time. After all, your brain is wired to keep you safe. The problem is your brain's bias toward the familiar and accessible may cause it to confuse safety with comfort. Anything new or difficult—a job interview, speaking in public, an exam, learning a new skill, or a first date—can all bring about fear.

Fear can disguise itself as perfectionism, procrastination, unassertiveness, or shutting down. Unchecked fear may cause you to isolate from social interactions or avoid challenges that could benefit you in the long run. When fear becomes habitual, it causes your nervous system to react in a hyper- or hypoaroused state.

There's an acronym for this kind of fear: *false evidence appears real.* When you're not in danger and not sure whether you are feeling your intuition or fear, ask yourself: Is your nervous system in a hyper- or hypoaroused state of mobilization or immobilization? If so, do the "Coming into Safety" practice before you precede.

Write down your fear.

_____

_____

How likely is it that your fear will come true? Think of it on a spectrum, with 1 being unlikely and 10 being guaranteed. You can come back to this once your worry has passed to see if your prediction was accurate.

_____

Is your fear based on thoughts, feelings, or both? Ideally you want to draw from the wisdom of your mind-body, not just your brain.

_____

Do a few belly breaths and drop your focus away from your mind into your heart and gut. Can you sense an inner knowing of what's most likely to happen if you act or don't act on your fear?

_____

_____

If you find it hard to do this and fear's still present, it's likely fear's running the show. We'll explore intuition, but first a little more about fear.

The way to free yourself from the grip of fear and gain access to your inner wisdom is to face it. Look at your fear and move forward with creative solutions. In *Emotional Agility,* Susan David (2016) writes, "Abandon the idea of being fearless, and instead walk directly into your fears, with your values as your guide, toward what matters to you. Courage is not an absence of fear: courage is fear walking" (242). Feeling fear is human. Conquering your fear will make you feel courageous, empowered, and proud. As my wise friend Michaela explained, fear does not have to remain inside of you. Take your fear by the hand and let it walk next to you.

Panic Strategies

Panic is the fear of anxiety. It arises when we fear that the feelings and sensations of anxiety will overtake us. Panic is a symptom of hyperarousal that can cause your heart to race, your breathing to speed up, you to break into a sweat, the desire to run or escape, you to feel like you're going to die, or you to feel like you're losing it. Rest assured, a panic attack is not deadly. Although it seems endless when you're having an attack, the discomfort lasts only for a short time. Remind yourself: "If I panic, I panic. It's unfortunate, but not horrific."

Here are some steps to help alleviate panic. Since you don't think as clearly when triggered or panicked, consider taking a picture of these steps and storing it in your phone so you have it available when needed or download a copy at http://newharbinger.com/46509.

- Acknowledge that you're having a panic attack. Accept the reality: while it's very uncomfortable, you won't die from a panic attack.

- Tell someone you trust that you're having a panic attack. This can relieve pressure.

- Take deeper slower breaths, focusing on long exhalations. Inhale for a count of three; exhale for a count of five. Shallow breath can be or represent something held in.

- If you're overbreathing (tingling, faintness, giddiness, heart palpations), practice controlled breathing by taking smooth, slow, regular, and fairly shallow breaths. Breathe in through your nose and out through your mouth in regular in-out cycles. Twelve per minute is often helpful, but find your own comfortable breathing rhythm.

- Remember "fear" means *false evidence appears real.*

- Anxiety is incompatible with relaxation. Come into mindful presence; open your awareness to the fullness of each moment through your senses. Being present will facilitate choice. Choice keeps us from feeling stuck or feeling like a victim.

- Don't deny what you're feeling. Instead learn to flow with it. Picture yourself a surfer and ride the wave of panic. It will go away sooner than later.

Some of the things that can trigger a panic attack are overwhelming feelings of fear, not having the skills to calm down your distressing emotions, trying hard to suppress implicit and explicit traumatic memories, and flashbacks. The sooner you catch a panic attack, the less likely it is to spiral out of control. Try answering the following questions when your nervous system has calmed down after a panic attack.

What physical and emotional reactions indicated that you were becoming anxious?

_____

_____

Try to identify what happened just before those cues. What was the trigger?

_____

_____

What trigger strategies (chapter 4) helped or might have helped to ease your distress?

_____

_____

_____

You don't have to be the one person who's in perfect control of their anxious moments. Shaming or judging yourself for what you're feeling will only make it worse. Bring in your self-compassion practice as needed. If panic attacks become chronic, seek help in resolving the underlying emotional conflict.

Learning to Listen to Your Intuition

Intuition can show up as a deep gut feeling, a sense of knowing what's right or wrong, an inner knowing of a direction or course of action to take, or a sense of energy trying to move you in a certain direction. Author Shakti Gawain (2000) writes, "As we learn to listen to our intuitive feelings and act on them, we are truly learning to follow our own energy as it moves and rests. When we are receptive and responsive to this flow, it feels like the life-force is moving us in an exquisite dance" (88).

Although feelings of uncertainty or risk can accompany intuition, most often you'll feel more like you're in a flow state, experiencing a sense of synchronicity or a feeling of being in the right place at the right time doing the right thing.

As you develop your intuition, it can be helpful to notice if following an intuitive hit brings a greater sense of aliveness and if ignoring it results in any feelings of numbness, depression, or loss of energy. You can also ask your intuition for guidance, for a clear signal if this is the right choice, or if not, to block it in some way. Your answer might come internally, such as a feeling of energy moving or not, a sense of knowing what direction to take, or an external sign like a song, word, or number that keeps showing up.

In *Developing Intuition*, Gawain (2000) explains one of the most difficult challenges can be when our intuition is telling us not to act: "We may have an idea about something we think we should be doing, and we find that there's simply no energy in it. We try to make ourselves do it, but it just doesn't work" (87). Self-doubt may arise before we recognize life's trying to convey that this isn't the best course of action at this time. Gawain goes on to say, "Intuition never guides us with an authoritarian or critical edge" (98). It doesn't push us to do anything that we're really not ready to do, it never makes us feel guilty about anything, nor does it lead us to do anything that isn't good for us.

To help decipher intuition from fear, notice if it feels emotionally charged or if your nervous system is in a hypo- or hyperaroused state. If so, ask yourself if this is a familiar trigger, such as the fear of rejection or abandonment. Say for instance, you fear making the wrong choice when it comes to dating. You might be trying to decipher whether it's intuition or fear telling you that the person isn't good for you. The best thing to do in this case is to ground and center yourself; then take slow deep yet gentle breaths as you calm your nervous system. You want to slow down your mind, go inward, and feel the stillness. Don't try to turn off the mind. That will make it fight to be heard. Just let it recede into the background. Ideally, you'll draw on both your intellect and your intuitive awareness in a harmonious manner. Once calm, check back in, ask your question, and see what your intuition has to say. Accurate intuitions are often compassionate, synchronistic, neutral or somewhat impersonal, and void of emotional charge.

Your intuition is finetuned to your individual needs in any given moment. Learn to trust it and draw on it. It can help you reach your highest potential and will reward you with a feeling of enlivenment and openness within your heart and soul.

PRACTICE: Tapping in to Intuition

If you deny, tune out, or ignore your intuition, it becomes blocked. Privileging the mind over the body also blocks it. Creativity, meditation, and guided imagery help slow you down and get you into your body where intuition lives. Gawain (2000) compares listening to, trusting, and acting on your intuitive inner guidance to an art form, "Like any other art or discipline, it requires a certain commitment. It is an ongoing process in which we are always being challenged to move to a deeper level of self-trust" (141). Learning to sense your inner knowing and trust in what comes through must be cultivated; at the same time, you may be doing so without realizing it.

Have you ever had an intuitive hit, gut feeling, or strong sense of inexplicitly knowing something? How did you feel it? Did you follow it, and what was the outcome?

_____

_____

_____

_____

Have you ever been afraid to follow an intuitive hit, gut feeling, or strong sense of knowing? What were the specific fears that prevented you from following your intuition?

_____

_____

_____

In retrospect, do you think you made the best choice? Is there anything you would like to have done differently? Be sure not to judge yourself for where you were at and what resources you had available to you at the time.

_____

_____

_____

Choose a period of time (a few days, a week, a month) to commit to trusting and following your intuition. Write in a journal any fears you come up against and the outcomes you experience.

PRACTICE: Intuition Break

Psychologist Rollo May reportedly said, "It is amazing how many hints and guides and intuitions for living come to the sensitive person who has ears to hear what his body is saying." This practice can help you slow down and hear what your body is saying as you tune in to your intuition.

- Begin by taking a few minutes to get comfortable and to ground. Then close or softly focus your eyes and follow the breath inward.

- Ask your intuition for support or guidance, and remain open to receive it however it shows up.

- Tune in to all of your senses. What do you smell or taste, hear, or see in your mind's eye? Note any colors or shapes

- What sensations do you notice in your body?

- Invite your reasoning mind to recede into the background as you gently shift into a deeper state of consciousness, sensing deeper and deeper into your inner truth and knowing.

- Imagine that you're following your own energy, trusting the life-force moving within you, creatively speaking and living your truth.

- Stay with it as long as you would like. Then give gratitude for your inner knowing, your intuition. When you're ready, gently open your eyes and come back into the room. Take a few minutes to write down what you experienced.

_____

_____

_____

_____

If you continue to show up in relation to your intuition, it will continue to open and support you. Next we'll explore another important skill that helps keep you safe: the ability to sense into, maintain, communicate, and assert boundaries.

CHAPTER 6

Boundaries Are an Ongoing Process of Choice

Inherent in being a survivor was the violation of physical and psychological boundaries. It wasn't safe or physiologically possible for you to have imposed a firmer boundary at the time or you would have. Your boundaries were not respected. Instead, they were ignored, breached, and shattered. As a result, you may struggle to set healthy boundaries. It's even possible you've internalized the unjust implication given that you didn't have the right to have and enforce a boundary.

Yet everything has a boundary—a line or parameter that designates where one thing ends and another begins. A cell has a membrane that forms a boundary, just as your skin is a boundary, letting things in and out as needed to support and sustain life. Relationally, you're continuously navigating and negotiating boundaries whether intentionally or not. Boundaries help protect you from being mistreated and let others know how you would like to be treated. They create healthy physical and emotional personal space and promote self-agency, allowing your actions to align with your values rather than doing what someone else wants you to do or being who someone else wants you to be.

Ideally your boundaries are elastic and flexible, shifting from moment to moment, automatically and intuitively adjusting according to your preferences and needs. The problem is, a lot of us were never modeled healthy boundaries. As a child you learned about boundaries from your parent(s) or primary caregiver, who set boundaries in an attempt to keep you safe. You had no choice, control, or understanding over whether you were modeled healthy boundaries or not. Children have to be given limits, but many children are shamed without repair or punished as they try to assert healthy boundaries. In order to survive and adapt, you may have built walls around you or learned to do what others wanted at the expense of taking care of yourself. You may have even felt responsible for the happiness of a parent or family member as you learned to ignore your own limitations, needs, and desires.

How were boundaries modeled to you as a child? For instance, when you were told no, were you given an explanation as to why, were you allowed to ask why, or were you allowed to voice your opinion without being shamed or punished?

_____

_____

_____

_____

How might healthier boundaries have been modeled to you?

_____

_____

_____

All of your boundaries, even the unhealthy ones, were survival resources at some point in your life. The thing is, you'll pay a price if you don't learn to set healthy boundaries moving forward. You need healthy boundaries to clearly convey *yes* and *no;* without them, you may feel used or coerced even when others have no intention of taking advantage of you and would respect your boundaries if you set them (Ogden and Fisher 2015). The capacity to set boundaries is essential to feeling a sense of empowerment. Learning to say no with your body and words can be difficult at first. It's common to struggle with a sense of guilt, but you'll soon find relief in no longer doing what you don't want to do.

Can you think of any current situations in which you want to say no but are having a hard time doing so?

_____

_____

_____

Don't try setting new boundaries just yet. There's a lot more to explore before taking that step. Let's take a look at some of the types of boundaries and the ways we set them.

Types of Boundaries

Personal boundaries include the limits and rules you set for yourself within relationships. Categories of personal boundaries include but are not limited to:

- Physical: Personal space and physical touch. Examples: You decide how close another can get to you, how much privacy or time alone you need, and if it's okay to give you a hug.

- Emotional: Your right to your feelings, when to share, and how much. Examples: It's not okay for others to invalidate how you're feeling or for you to be responsible for others' feelings, yet it's important that you respect other's feelings.

- Intellectual: Thoughts and ideas. Examples: It's not okay for others to criticize you for your thoughts or ideas, to take credit for another's ideas, or for someone else to take credit for yours.

- Sexual: Consent, limitations, and desires. Examples: You choose when it's okay for your partner(s) to touch you, where you're comfortable with your partner touching you, and the quality of that touch.

- Material: Money and possessions. Examples: It's your right to be paid by your employer for your work, to spend your money however you choose, and to loan or not loan your money or possessions.

- Time: Demands on or respect for your time and how you spend it. Examples: You choose to not let others sway you into doing something you don't want to do, to not put in unpaid or unwanted overtime at work, and to allow enough time in your day for self-care.

- Spiritual: Your right to believe in what you want. Examples: You have the freedom to hold different spiritual beliefs than your partner(s) or family, to worship where you want, and to practice your beliefs how you want.

- Nonnegotiable: Boundaries you absolutely must have in order to feel safe. These can come from any of the previous categories. Examples: You have the right to walk away from a relationship when someone has betrayed your trust by breaking an agreement, not following through with a commitment, or refusing to agree to your boundary in the first place. It's only nonnegotiable if you've clearly stated it and you enforce it.

Another way we can view boundaries is by how our bodies, thoughts, and emotions are making or not making a boundary at any given time. Boundaries are fluid and flexible. For instance, when you're tired, stressed, or fearful, you're likely to set firmer boundaries than when you're feeling relaxed and energized. If you've ever been out in nature, think back to how it feels, that sense of connection to something greater than yourself, that expansiveness you can feel with your entire being. This feeling of an open or expansive boundary only happens when you feel safe and resourced in the moment.

Can you remember a time when your boundaries felt expansive? As you bring that memory to mind, stay with it for a bit. Take note of what you're experiencing with each of your senses. What sensations are you aware of? What feelings and thoughts are present?

_____

_____

_____

_____

_____

Boundaries can be porous, ridged, or healthy and flexible. If you tend to avoid others or keep them at a distance, your boundaries are considered rigid. If you tend to get overly involved or take on others' feelings, your boundaries are considered porous. You likely have a mix of different boundary types. For example, you might have healthy boundaries at work, porous boundaries with your close friends, and a mix of healthy, rigid, and porous with your family members. The following lists give a general overview of rigid, porous, and healthy boundaries.

Rigid boundaries. When boundaries are rigid, people tend to:

- be overly protective of personal information
- be unlikely to ask for help
- seem detached, even with romantic partners
- avoid intimacy and close relationships
- keep others at a distance out of fear of rejection

Porous boundaries. When boundaries are porous, people tend to:

- overshare personal information
- have difficulty saying no to others' requests

- be dependent on the opinions of others

- be overly involved with others' problems

- comply with others out of fear of rejection

Healthy boundaries. When boundaries are healthy, people tend to:

- not over- or undershare personal information

- be accepting when others say no to them

- value their own opinion

- know their personal wants and needs

- never compromise their values for others

Although you may have a tendency toward one boundary type, you probably have a mix of healthy, porous, and rigid depending on how you're feeling in the moment, the situation you're in, and how you feel about the person(s) you're with. If your boundaries are healthy, you can say no to others when you choose to and you're comfortable opening up to intimacy and close relationships when you want to. For further exploration of your relational boundaries, download the "Relational Boundary Exploration" worksheet at http://newharbinger.com/46509.

Sensing into Your Boundaries

After suffering a sexual assault, many of your boundaries were shattered. When your boundaries are shattered, it's as though your energy is leaking out of you. You can't change or strengthen your boundaries with your thoughts alone; it will only add to your stress. To strengthen your boundaries, you'll have to sense them in your body. To become skilled at healthy boundary-making, you'll need to tune in to the information you're receiving from your body, paying close attention to what your sensations and emotions are signaling in relation to your preferences, rights, needs, and desires, and then communicate this nonverbally, and when called for, verbally.

When you listen to the cues, your body's visceral and muscular sensations will inform you. In previous chapters you've learned to bring awareness to sensations. Now you'll begin to decipher what they're telling you in relation to your needs for closeness or distance. If for instance, you take a deeper breath or you notice a sense of calm wash over you, it might feel comfortable to move physically or emotionally closer. This is the warm, fuzzy feeling you get when a pet or person you love is close to you. When you're needing distance, your body might signal you to make a boundary with shallow breathing; your stomach, chest, throat, or pelvic floor constricting; an anxious feeling; or a desire to pull away. These sensations may be familiar if you know anyone who tends to take without giving, continuously complains, criticizes, or feels like an energy vampire.

There are times you may experience seemingly contradictory feelings, such as expansive warmth in your solar plexus and at the same time feel constriction in your throat. How do you know what to do then? Begin by distinguishing what sensations are what. For instance, you might know that you get anxious when you begin to get close to someone. This doesn't mean you don't want to or should not get close. It might just mean you're feeling vulnerable about getting close. Conversely, you might get a sense that something is not quite right or that you should not trust this person. In that case, notice the sensation and how you feel it in your body. The two situations may feel similar, but they're not the same. With the anxiety, you may want to relax and acknowledge the fear without judgment, and when you get the sense that something is not quite right, you may want to trust your instincts, disengage, and make sure you're safe.

In the practices that follow, you'll learn how to be mindful of what's showing up in your body as you connect to a felt sense of your boundaries.

PRACTICE: Nonverbal Boundaries

As a vulnerable infant, you learned to communicate boundaries through facial expressions, vocalizations, and movements, such as turning or pushing away. Think about some of the ways you continue to make a boundary with your body. Try acting out the boundaries in the list below. Notice what sensations, feelings, and thoughts are alive in you as you try them on.

- Cross your arms.

- Avert your gaze.

- Sneer, scowl, or frown.

- Tighten or clench your jaw.

- Turn your head away.

- Lean back and away.

- Push away with your hands and arms.

- Make a stop motion.

- Walk away.

How do you tend to physicalize nonverbal boundaries? What are some of your go-tos?

_____

_____

Why do you like these particular boundaries?

_____

_____

Are they usually successful in communicating the message you want to get across?

_____

_____

How did it feel to physicalize the unfamiliar actions?

_____

_____

Are there any you would like to incorporate into your nonverbal boundary setting?

_____

_____

When the posture and movement of your body aligns with your words, a clear and decisive message is conveyed. This supports and strengthens your boundary-making. The following boundary practice can help you feel a sense of protection.

PRACTICE: The Egg Boundary

Energy can be seen as the motivating force that drives everything. The subtle body, or aura, is an energy field that surrounds the body and conveys information about what's taking place inside of the body. In this practice, you'll work with that subtle energy.

Have you ever felt like someone was standing too close, like they're in your space? Perhaps it was a stranger talking too close at a party, someone in a line, or a person on a train or bus who was so close that they brushed up against you. This exercise will help you recognize when someone is too close before it feels like they are invading your space. This will help you sense into, work with, and draw on the energetic boundaries that extend beyond the surface of your skin. For this, we use the analogy of an egg: your skin and all that's contained within is the yolk, the egg white is the aura or energy you can sense and feel into, and the shell is where you feel a sense of boundary. In this case the shell's not fragile like an egg's, but rather malleable, like Silly Putty (the clay toy that comes in an egg-shaped container), since your boundaries are flexible and fluid.

- Find a place to comfortably stand with several feet of space surrounding you. Next, find your center by gently swaying your body from side to side then back and forth. Notice where you feel most grounded and supported; then take a few belly breaths.

- Rub your hands or the tips of your fingertips together to generate some heat. Now bring your palms together, a few inches apart, and see if you can feel a subtle sense of energy, heat, or a magnetic feeling emanating between your hands. Gently move your hands a little closer, a little further apart, and then closer again, noticing what subtle sensations arise.

- Now imagine or visualize an inverted egg-shaped boundary surrounding you. You can think of this as the place where you recognize too close, or where your energetic aura, the distinctive atmosphere that seems to surround or be generated by you, is strongest.

- Reach out with your palms and begin to sense and feel the outer edges of this boundary. You may feel a sense of energy dissipating, a pressure, or tingling. Try to stay present and go slow; this can be very subtle.

- Notice what sensations are present as you continue to feel into this boundary all around and above you. Is there anywhere on the shell that feels vulnerable, as though it's too thin or there's a hole, anywhere it feels strong, and anywhere it feels too rigid?

- If you found an area that feel's vulnerable, try moving some boundary from thicker areas of the shell over to this area, filling it in, or try pushing with both hands into this area to strengthen the boundary. You can also push into a ridged boundary to help it become more flexible.

Be sure not to judge what you found. Just like with the fight-flight-freeze response, there are good reasons why your boundaries have formed the way they have. Practice sensing into your boundary, feeling it around you as a subtle form of protection when you wake up or before you leave your home.

Putting the Egg Boundary into Practice

My friend Michaela first introduced me to a version of the egg boundary. I practiced feeling into it for a few weeks and then didn't give it much thought. Months later, after a long day of psychotherapy training, I was traveling from Berkeley to San Francisco on public transportation. It was late, and the train was almost empty. As I boarded, I saw there were only two passengers at opposite ends, both men. I sat down in a seat across and over from one of them. As we pulled away from the platform, he began staring at me and mumbling graphicly threatening statements. I felt vulnerable and drained from the day and at a loss as to what to do. He was likely psychotic, and I sensed that if I moved seats, he may follow or become more confrontational.

Suddenly the image of the egg appeared, only with knives facing outward along the entire surface. I was momentarily startled. I'm not a violent person, and the image disturbed me. Within seconds, I let go of the judgment as my entire being connected to an empowered sense of boundary. Simultaneously, I heard and felt the energy of the words "Don't fuck with me." At the very moment I embodied this boundary, the man stood up and exited the car for the next one over. A wave of relief moved through my body as I felt my nervous system moving back toward safety.

About five minutes later, the same man returned. He stood close above me starring down and again began mumbling threats. This time I intentionally visualized the egg with knives facing outward as I embodied the boundary, and once again he immediately walked away exiting the car. I didn't see him again and made it home safely.

This is just one of many ways you can use the egg boundary. I'm not suggesting you walk around with this level of boundary, nor that you rely on this boundary alone to keep you safe, but if you're ever in a situation where you need it and you've practiced feeling into it, it's quite powerful.

Decorating the Egg

There are many other wonderful uses for the egg boundary. When people say unkind things, you can use the egg to keep their words out there, to not let them in. Simply visualize their words hitting the outer shell and bouncing off the egg. Then imagine their words landing wherever you'd like. After hearing an unmindful friend make the horrific comment, "I'd rather die than be raped," Renee shared, "I had my egg up. I felt something like what could have been a dagger, but it bounced off." Renee was impressively successful in preventing the triggering remark from hijacking her nervous system into a sympathetic or dorsal vagal response.

Another great use of the egg boundary is for empaths and those who tend toward porous boundaries. If you're highly sensitive with a tendency to take on others' feelings, you can visualize the egg covered in mirrors, like a disco ball. This allows others' energy (and words) to reflect off the egg and back to them. Rather than taking on and feeling others' suffering, this practice creates enough separation for you to send them compassion, if you choose.

The egg boundary can also be used to contain. Renee, who struggled with feelings of pain in and around her heart after being sexually assaulted, used the imagery of the egg whenever she felt herself begin to dissociate. She shared how the boundary helped bring her back into her body, "When I feel the pain in my heart, my mind starts wandering [dissociating], it will hit the container [eggshell] then move away. My mind says, *No not now.*" The boundary helped Renee feel contained and realize it was safe to return to her body.

Get creative with the egg. Imagine whatever you want on the outer shell or keep it simple, reflecting your mood and whatever type of boundary is called for at the time. You can create a mantra, such as, "May you protect me and only allow in what nourishes my soul." I was touched when one client shared that she fills her egg white with little hearts, what a great way to practice self-compassion!

Can you think of anything you would like to add to the egg when making a boundary?

_____

_____

_____

PRACTICE: **The Yarn Boundary**

For this practice you'll need a ball of yarn, string, or rope. If you don't have any of these, you can get creative with several charging cords, belts, pillows, books, or anything else to indicate a boundary. You can do this exercise on your own, but it's even better if you have a friend or partner to work with.

- Begin as you did with the "Egg Boundary," grounding and centering yourself, rubbing your palms together, and then feeling into the space around you until you get a sense of where your external boundaries are located at this moment. Take your time to mindfully notice how close would feel too close.

- Now take your yarn, or other material you have to work with, and place it all the way around yourself in a circle, oval, or whatever form it takes, to indicate where your boundaries are located. Notice if the boundary is further away in some directions and closer to you in others.

- Once you're surrounded with your now-tangible boundary, imagine someone walking up to the edge of it. Would it feel too close, too far away, or just right, and what tells you this? Where in your body do you feel it, and what sensations are present? For instance, does your breathing or heart rate change? Do you feel constriction in your stomach, heart center, or throat?

- Try stepping outside of your boundary, take note of how this feels, then step back inside, and notice if you feel any different.

- Adjust your boundary to reflect the information your body's giving you, and again imagine someone walking up to your boundary and around it, paying close attention to what sensations are alive in you.

- If you have a friend to work with, ask them to walk up to the edge of your boundary as you listen to what your body's telling you. Adjust your boundary if needed. Direct your friend to slowly move a few feet at a time around your designated boundary, pausing long enough to allow you take note of what's too close, too far, and just right, and what tells you this. Where in your body do you feel it? If you have an intense response of too close, ask your friend to step back until you're comfortable, and then readjust your boundary. If needed, do "Coming into Safety," and then continue the exercise on your own.

What physical sensations indicated too close, too far away, and just right?

_____

_____

_____

How did it feel to step outside of your boundary?

_____

_____

Was your boundary closer to some parts of your body and further away from others, and if so where?

_____

_____

_____

It's not unusual to underestimate the amount of distance that designates your boundary in any given moment. I've rarely seen anyone overestimate it. You may have noticed an area, such as directly in front of you, directly behind you, or as you're losing your peripheral vision, where you need more of a boundary. This can reflect the direction from which you experienced a past trauma or a place where your boundaries may be a little more vulnerable. Knowing this can be useful information. For instance, it's helped many of my clients determine where to best position themselves in meetings and social gatherings, and several have drawn on their body's intelligence for placement during their wedding vows. If one side felt vulnerable, that was the side that faced their partner. This way, their more boundaried or protected side faced out to the audience.

Can you think of a way you might apply the information gained from this practice?

_____

_____

_____

Remember there's no right or wrong when it comes to your boundaries, only what is right for you. The boundary exercises that follow will help you get in touch with an embodied sense of saying no when needed.

PRACTICE: **Yes, No, and Maybe**

Boundaries are an ongoing process of making choice, and much of that choice will fall within the space between yes and no. In this exercise you'll notice (1) how your body signals yes and how this informs you when you're in agreement with something, (2) how you recognize when your body is telling you no and how this indicates you're not in alignment with something, and (3) how you acknowledge when you're in the space between yes or no, *maybe*. A maybe could mean negotiating, compromising, or simply needing more time to get comfortable with your yes or no.

- Sitting or standing, take several deep gentle breaths as you ground and center yourself. Close your eyes or bring them to a soft focus by engaging your peripheral vision. Think of something positive that you've wanted to say or have said yes to. When you feel ready, say the word "yes" outload a few times. Notice how your whole body feels. What sensations are present?

_____

_____

Try saying yes again with a loud voice. Does your body feel the word, and if so, where? Do you feel a sense of expansion or contraction? Can you sense your yes in the energy field extending beyond your body?

_____

_____

_____

- Next bring to mind something you wanted to say or have said no to. Say the word "no" in a loud voice several times. What signals and sensations do you notice when you feel into no? Is it a feeling in your jaw, throat, heart center, stomach, or pelvis?

_____

_____

_____

- Say it again focusing inward and using your full voice. How do you know when it's not feeling right? Do you notice your breathing getting short, your stomach constricting, or your body wanting to move away? Do you sense your no in the energy field extending beyond your body? If it's uncomfortable for you to say no, how do you feel this in your body?

_____

_____

_____

- If there's a boundary you're unsure of, think about the range of choice between your yes and your no. Does your boundary fall somewhere within the space of maybe? Try bringing the boundary to mind then saying yes as you notice what's alive in your body. Next, repeat "no" a few times. How do you feel your no? Is your body's response bringing you closer to yes or no? Write down your observations.

_____

_____

_____

Your Words, Tone, and Voice

Your words and tone convey an energy and imprint of meaning that resonates within your body. When you're aligned with your yes, it can feel expansive, like an opening and increased energy; yes is receptive. Your no might feel like a wall, shield, or armor somewhere in or near your body; no is a boundary. Opening to yes usually takes less energy than saying no, but it's not always what's best for you. If you say yes when you don't want to, it will usually cost you more in the long run. At the same time, you don't want to close yourself off by making no your go-to response. As you draw on your body-mind's innate wisdom, you'll become more receptive to and authentic with the boundaries you choose to define.

Your voice is vital in making a boundary. It's the means with which you make choices and speak your truth to the world. If you're a survivor of molestation or sexual assault, your voice may have been silenced. You were likely paralyzed by fear. You may have been manipulated. You may have been told it happened because you're special, bad, or worthless; it was your fault; it was a secret; or no one would believe you. You may have been threatened with further harm to yourself or those you love if you spoke your truth. Sadly, many survivors muster up the courage to tell a family member or friend only to be accused of lying. The heavy weight of internalized shame is yet another way survivors are silenced. Because of this, it might be hard for you to vocalize your boundaries. The thing is, when your physical boundaries are not respected, requests, and sometimes more forceful demands, need to be vocalized.

PRACTICE: Projecting Your Voice

To speak your truth, you'll need to get comfortable aiming your voice out into the world. This practice, inspired by Paul Linden, PhD, (2004) will help you build that skill.

- Begin by getting a box of tissues and then find a comfortable place to lie down. You can place a pillow under your head if you want.

- Now place a piece of tissue across your face. Inhale a full deep breath; then blow on the tissue as you exhale.

- Did the tissue fly up into the air above you? If so, great. This is how your breath and muscles align to project your voice out into the world. If not, adjust your breath. Think of the belly breaths from chapter 1. Make sure your inhale is fully filling your lungs as your abdomen gently expands outward, and then exhale as your belly pulls inward, blowing up and out as you aim the tissue above.

- If you're having a hard time, take a moment to relax your body—your hands, feet, shoulders, and abdomen. Then do several relaxed belly breaths, and try again.

- Once you've got it, try speaking while engaging the same muscles, and then speak again sitting or standing. When speaking with others, you won't need to be as forceful, unless you need to communicate a firm boundary.

Did it feel like you projected your words out into the world?

_____

_____

How do you imagine your message might be received when you aim your words out like this?

_____

_____

Is there any part of you that found this difficult? If so, why do you think that is?

_____

_____

_____

_____

It can be uncomfortable getting used to something new, even if it's good for you. Play with it and see if you can become comfortable aiming your words out into the world.

PRACTICE: Stop Boundary

For this boundary exercise, you'll need to stand on one side or corner of a room, ideally facing across from a door on the opposite side or corner of the room. You're going to imagine a person you know opening the door, entering, and beginning to walk toward you. You didn't invite them into your space, so you're going to make a boundary and tell them to stop, that you're not okay with them entering or coming any closer. How you respond will depend in part on who you imagine, how close you are, and how much you trust them. Don't imagine anyone who's a real threat to you. If any fear arises, picture it as a solid object, and then visualize the fear lifting away from your body and dissolving into the atmosphere.

- Ground and center yourself; take a few deep yet gentle breaths. Then, when you're ready, imagine the person you chose entering the room.

- Extend your hands and arms out in front of you and say, "Stop! I'm not inviting you into my space. You need to leave." Feel free to change the wording to make it more authentic, but do include "stop." Now say it loudly and with your hands, like you mean it.

- Notice how it felt in your body. Were you convincing? Did you speak from a place of empowerment?

- If not try it again, but first notice where strength resides in your body. Perhaps your strength is in your thighs, abdomen, back, shoulders, or arms. If you can't find that sense of strength now, think of a time that you've felt it. Perhaps a time when you achieved something you're proud of, excelled at a sport, or stood up for a friend. See if you can connect with that sense of strength in yourself now.

- After trying it again, how did it feel? Did it come from a more empowered place within you? What did you do differently?

- Try it a few more times until you can feel the power of your *stop* with your entire being.

If this exercise was difficult for you, try it again using what you've learned from the "Projecting Your Voice" practice. Take some time now to reflect on your experience.

_____

_____

_____

_____

_____

If this practice was hard for you, you're not alone. Most everyone I work with struggles to make this boundary at first. As previously mentioned, most girls in this culture are conditioned to be agreeable from around the time they hit puberty, and some boys also learn that they have to be agreeable to avoid rejection and bullying. As a result, it can feel wrong within your entire being to make a firm and decisive physical and verbal boundary such as "stop." Don't judge or shame yourself for this. You were a good student in learning the lessons that were being taught. The lesson was flawed, not you.

Breath, muscle tone, and posture align to create your unique voice. With this practice, like many of the others, you're teaching you're body a new skill. If it doesn't yet feel authentic, come back to it in a day or two and try again for as many days as it takes until you strengthen your connection with it, allowing yourself to embody your stop and your no.

Consent Is an Ongoing Process

Sexual consent is an agreement or permission between two (legally of age) participants to engage in a sexual activity. If there're more than two participants, consent needs to be given and received with each and may differ from one person to another. The laws on consent vary from state to state and country to country. To read what's legal in your state, go to http://rainn.org and search the site using this phrase: "the laws in your state: [name of state]."

If you give your consent once, it doesn't mean that it's ongoing or that you've consented to increased sexual contact, even with a partner or spouse. For instance, if you consent to a kiss, it doesn't mean you consented to being touched on other parts of your body, and if you consent to being intimately touched, it doesn't mean you consented to intercourse or that you've given permission for this person to touch you again in the future.

When not stated explicitly, boundaries and consent can be very confusing. People have different ideas and cultural conditioning regarding what's acceptable. Unfortunately, some people haven't learned the importance of asking for consent or don't respect others enough to ask. Don't wait for potential partners to initiate a conversation. Let them know you'll ask for consent and that you expect them do the same.

You might find yourself in a situation where you gave consent, and then thoughts and sensations arise signaling that you're no longer comfortable with your decision. If this happens, it's important to remember you have the right to withdraw consent at any time. If you choose to withdraw consent, be sure to communicate this verbally in order to prevent any confusion.

Consent is a boundary, and as stated, boundaries are an ongoing process of making choice. As you heal sexually, you're likely to experience moments of awkwardness, discomfort, and fear as implicit fragments of the trauma surface and unconscious beliefs play out. When this happens, it will feel even more challenging to make a clear choice. Be gentle with yourself as you continue to pay attention to your boundaries. You have to get to know them before you can communicate them to others. A stronger connection to your yes, no, and maybe will continue to develop as you learn to check in with and listen to your body. If you get a maybe, slow down and wait until you have a clearer sense of "Yes," "I'm willing to try," "No," or "No, and don't ask me again."

Unintegrated trauma can further complicate consent due to potential influence from unconscious trauma responses. For instance, a survivor might become aroused in ways that are self-destructive by unconsciously reenacting their trauma. With this in mind psychotherapist Jessica Hicks, MA, MA, LMFT (2019) developed the Dynamic Sexual Consent Assessment Tool, a series of four questions that can help deepen your response when considering consent, which you can also find online at http://newharbinger.com/46509.

The Dynamic Sexual Consent Assessment Tool Questions

- *Is this YES ego-syntonic?* Does consent align with my values and my innate sense of myself?

- *What age is my YES?* How old do I feel when I say "yes," and is my consent emanating from a younger version of myself?

- *Where do I feel the YES in my body?* Is consent resonant and consistent across the domains of my head, heart, and sexual center?

- *Is there any conflict inherent in my YES?* Do I notice any signs or evidence of misgivings when I assert my consent?

You might want to take a picture of these questions or add them to the notes on your phone so you have them available when you need them. If necessary, excuse yourself so you have the space and privacy to answer each question before consenting.

When you choose a partner, make sure they respect your boundaries, as you respect theirs, and that their actions align with their words. You need to be willing to enforce your stated boundaries if they're crossed, for example by telling your partner that they've crossed your boundary and you're no longer in the mood or by asking them to leave. Get to know your limits since tuning in to and listening to your body can become impaired when drinking alcohol or using mood-altering substances. Finally, be sure to respect your boundaries in the same way you're asking others to respect them.

— *Story:* Bodily Autonomy

Mia, a molestation survivor, was frustrated with her partner, especially his ongoing bids for intimacy. We began working on boundaries as she learned to feel into and trust her yes, no, and maybe. Soon she started making requests of her partner involving things such as household chores and more importantly, requests and boundaries regarding intimacy. Some of her requests lead to further discussion and compromise; others were agreed to right away. Their relationship improved in many ways, but Mia still struggled at times with sexual boundaries.

One day she shared a realization when her partner hadn't been respecting her stated boundaries. Mia told him that she didn't feel like she had bodily autonomy, that it felt like her body belonged to him. To her surprise, he responded with compassion, letting her know that he didn't want her to feel this way. This led to the realization that she hadn't been enforcing her boundaries by restating them when her partner tested or forgot them, and people often will test them, especially when they're new. Instead Mia submitted and had gone along with what her partner initiated. As a result, she'd been harboring anger and resentment at him.

After Mia disclosed this to her partner, he asked if she wanted to go back to one of the first sexual boundaries she'd made: that she be the one to initiate intimacy. She said no, that she did not want to reinforce that boundary. Then she restated the boundaries she wanted to keep in place. Her partner agreed to respect these boundaries, and Mia left the conversation with a strong realization that she had power over her physical body. Although she'd always loved him, both getting clear on and communicating her boundaries led Mia to liking and respecting her partner more than ever.

Recognizing and Naming Your Needs

As illustrated in Mia's story, another aspect of making a boundary is the ability to make a request. It can be difficult to make requests when you're not used to doing so. The thing is, if you can't request what you need or desire, you're not likely to get it. Often people underestimate the importance of this skill until they begin to develop it and quickly realize how much they've been holding back.

Many people believe their partner, best friend, or family member should know how they feel and what they're needing without having to communicate it, yet others aren't capable of reading minds. The best chance you have of getting your needs met is to clearly request what you want from another. In order to formulate and communicate a request, you have to first get in touch with what you need. And to get in touch with what you need, you have to know what you're feeling.

Feelings. As simple as it sounds, accurately naming emotions can take some getting used to. We tend to have far more words available to judge, criticize, or insult than we have to clearly express our emotional state. That's because when difficult emotions surface, it sometimes seems easier to focus on the other person rather than connect with our own feelings.

See if you can get precise in describing your emotional state. For example, are you feeling confused, or would ambivalent, conflicted, or hesitant be more accurate? Try to get very specific in expressing how you're feeling without using words that describe thoughts, judgments, or interpretations. Refer to the list of emotions at http://newharbinger.com/46509, and feel free to add to it. (We'll dive more deeply into emotions in the next chapter.)

Needs. We all have needs. They help us feel safe, accepted, understood, healthy, and happy. When you identify your needs, the possibility of having them met is greatly increased. Marshal Rosenberg (2015), the founder of Nonviolent Communication (NVC), taught that when we judge, criticize, evaluate, or make interpretations of others, we're really expressing our needs in an alienating way. If you tell someone, "You don't understand me," what's actually being communicated is that your need to be understood isn't being met. Furthermore, if you express your needs in this way, others are more likely to respond with criticism.

No one person is responsible for meeting your needs, which can be met in many ways. For example, if you feel lonely, you might want to reach out to a friend for support. If your friend isn't available, you could spend time with your pet. If you don't have a pet, you can pick up a pillow and give it a big hug. You're responsible for how you feel and for your needs being met. This is personal empowerment.

Requests. In the example above, when reaching out to a friend, you may have made a request for their time and support. In making a request, be sure to state what you do need, not what you don't want, and try not to imply wrongness on the part of other people. You might include what you're feeling along with your request, such as, "I've been feeling kind of lonely since the assault. You're one of the few people I've felt safe with. Would you be open to a weekly meet up?"

Be careful not to put the other on the defensive. Avoid words that will place blame on them, such as, "You made me feel…" You also want to be mindful not to make a demand because demands leave the other person with two options: to rebel or to submit (Rosenburg 2015). Most people don't react well to feeling forced into either corner, so leave room for compromise whenever possible. Some boundaries will need to be firm demands, such as if your safety is threatened.

Ground and center yourself. Then ask yourself the following questions:

What are you feeling? What emotion is present?

_____

What need of yours is connected to the feeling you've identified?

_____

_____

Is this a need you can meet on your own? If so, how might you do that?

_____

_____

_____

Do you want to make a request? If so, how do you want to formulate it?

_____

_____

_____

Your feelings often result from how you choose to receive and perceive what others say and do as well as your individual needs and expectations in the moment. When you relate your feelings to your needs and share them, it helps strengthen your boundaries and opens the possibility for deeper connection.

When learning to formulate a request, you can first refer to the list of challenging emotions to hone in on and name what you're feeling. Be aware also that when expressing your feelings while making a request, some words tend to put the other person on the defense by placing blame. You can find these lists on the "Challenging Emotions List" handout at http://newharbinger.com/46509.

Setting a Boundary

Most of your boundary-setting work is done in the space between yes and no. So it's necessary to slow it down when you can and practice feeling into the range of possibility. It's common to overdo it at first, to be a little too rigid with your boundaries, or to revert back to people pleasing. As you gain experience, you'll settle into the sweet spot.

When you're ready to try setting a boundary, start with a small one (unless it involves your safety, then you need to start there). Then gradually build up to the more difficult ones. Be clear and direct. Resist any urge to apologize for your requests or boundaries, remembering that your feelings, thoughts, and needs are just as important as anyone else's. Expect some resistance from people who prefer things remain as is for their own benefit.

If you're worried conflict will arise, ask a friend or supportive family member to be there with you. What matters most is that you're able to safely advocate for yourself. To reduce anxiety, I suggest you write down or rehearse your requests and any boundaries you want or need to communicate. Here's a template:

I feel _____ when _____

_____

I'm requesting _____

_____

Some people in your life will push back as they witness this new side of you, while others may welcome it. If they push back or forget, you may need to repeat your boundary. If they refuse to honor your boundaries, you have the choice to physically and emotionally distance yourself or, if necessary, end the relationship. It's takes courage to show up for yourself as you risk disappointing others. Stay strong, and remind yourself that healthy boundaries are a form of self-agency, self-care, and protection.

Another way to courageously show up for yourself is through cultivating emotional intelligence, the topic of chapter 7.

CHAPTER 7

Strengthening Your Resilience with Emotional Intelligence

Your life is enriched by emotions. They add fullness and depth to all you experience. They're your body's instantaneous response to incoming internal and external messages, to information that can inform you, help you survive, and even help you thrive. Emotions can also be unreliable, clouding and confusing your perception of what you're experiencing in the moment due to painful unresolved attachment (relational) wounds and unintegrated trauma. Emotions can derail you, or they can inform and empower you.

Do you ever experience sudden emotions that feel out of control, such as those that arise when your nervous system goes into the fight-flight-freeze response? If so, describe what this feels like.

_____

_____

_____

These are the emotional responses that can sometimes be unreliable since your perspective can be skewed when you're in these states. When you're able to calm down and connect with some level of safety, your emotions will shift. You may look at the same situation and feel differently. Has this ever happened to you?

_____

_____

_____

Bringing awareness to your emotions and the messages they're trying to convey will help you respond to life's ups and downs in a more centered, thoughtful, and intentional manner.

Our emotions are states of feeling accompanied by physical and psychological changes that influence behavior. Bill Bowen (2013), founder of Psycho-Physical Therapy, explained: "Sensations are the DNA of emotions. Emotions are simply complex states informed by sensations and stimulated by thoughts." So emotions inform you through bodily sensations, and observing bodily sensations helps you identify what emotion you're feeling. You might feel butterflies in your stomach when nervous or excited, a constricted throat when afraid, a tight jaw when holding back feelings of anger, or flushed cheeks when embarrassed.

Are you aware of what sensations you feel when you're nervous, excited, afraid, angry, or embarrassed?

_____

_____

_____

If not, that's okay. We'll explore how to recognize emotions and sensations. Then we'll delve further into some common emotions that survivors experience moving forward.

Minimizing and Suppressing Emotions

As an infant, you learned which emotions generated negative reactions in your parent(s) or caregiver and how to minimize or suppress these emotions, whether positive or negative, in order to reduce painful feelings of shame, fear, and rejection. While this can help babies move toward a secure attachment with their parent(s) or to survive in the case of trauma and neglect, suppressing or burying emotions comes at a cost. Eventually these suppressed emotions will seep out in some other way, such as being ruled by negativity or shame, unexpectedly flying into explosive rage, feeling numb, or developing anxiety, depression, or even physical illness.

Are there any emotions you're aware of having to hide from others when you were a child?

_____

_____

_____

What was the cost of this on you?

_____

_____

_____

Boys in our culture learn by age four or five to suppress many of their emotions because of the misguided belief modeled by many adults and much of society that it's not masculine to show emotions. If you were a male child, you may have heard phrases such as "Get over it," or "Man up," and been shut down or ostracized when you became emotional. The cost of this to boys as they grow into adults is loss of connection because deep connection and intimacy require vulnerably sharing your feelings, thoughts, and beliefs.

Getting clear on your emotional state will bring more awareness to your experience, ultimately impacting your decisions and your future. We often don't realize the influence even a fleeting incidental emotional state can have on our decisions. When scanning your body with a nonjudgmental observing presence, you can pick up on sensations you'd otherwise miss, informing you about your emotions and bringing awareness to how those emotions are influencing your actions, which in turn influence your future.

You'll be more likely to offer something of value to the communication if you reflect on your visceral reactions to challenging conversations before responding. When emotions arise, especially unwelcome ones, if you make contact with yourself—not just up in your head but with the entirety of your experience—you'll discover more of the wisdom your body-mind and emotions contain. This doesn't always come naturally. The exercises in this chapter will help you learn this skill.

Acknowledging, Allowing, and Accepting Emotions

When you allow your emotions to inform you, you're able to observe how you're feeling while remaining present and maintaining perspective without getting swept away by past hurts or future fears. An emotion has an energetic reverberation, a wave form that flows through you. It rises up, peaks or crests, and then falls away. If the wave form of the emotion doesn't get to fulfill its expression, it remains in your body on a molecular level.

Learning to acknowledge, allow, and accept your emotions is very important because rejecting your thoughts, feelings, and sensations as wrong can lead to deep-rooted guilt and shame, increase the intensity and duration of the emotion, drain your energy, decrease your ability to problem solve, and negatively impact your relationships. Denying or resisting your unwelcome emotions will only strengthen them and ultimately, decrease your capacity to feel positive emotions.

PRACTICE: Acknowledge, Allow, Accept

You can learn to use an emotion's energy to help you move through an experience and grow from it. Bringing awareness to what you're feeling is the first step toward emotional intelligence.

- Begin by dropping your awareness into your body, feeling your weight on the chair or surface supporting you and your feet making contact with the floor.

- *Acknowledge.* Acknowledge what you're feeling, giving room for whatever emotion is present to be without judgment, criticism, or resistance. Do your best to simply observe and acknowledge. Once you've acknowledged what emotions are present, scan your body and locate where these emotions reside. Usually one area will call your attention strongly. If not, pick an area with a sensation you want to focus on.

- *Allow.* Observe any specific qualities to the sensation, such as tightening, constriction, empty, numb, heavy, tingly, hot, or cold. Take your time and just notice, again without judgment, where your attention's called and what's present. If your body wants to move, allow it the space to move. If you feel tense or constricted, visualize your breath gently touching and permeating the sensation of tension. If you feel overwhelmed, shift your focus back to grounding and contacting a sense of safety in your environment.

- *Accept.* After you've located and observed the sensation, notice what shape it takes. Now find the edges of the shape and see if you can soften around it, entering into that softness and giving it lots of space to simply be. Put aside any stories about yourself as you accept what is present at this time.

Once you've dropped into your body and brought awareness to the sensations accompanying your emotional state, it's helpful to identify and name your present feeling. This is important because it might not be the same emotion that you initially felt. As you mindfully observed sensations, you may have located a deeper underlying emotion, such as a sadness under the anger or a sense of shame beneath the anxiety, or perhaps you transitioned into another emotional state altogether.

As simple as it sounds, accurately naming emotions can take some getting used to. See if you can get precise in describing your emotional state. For help with this, refer to the "Challenging Emotions List" at http://newharbinger.com/46509.

What emotion was present for you in the last practice? Be as precise as possible.

_____

_____

What did you notice when you connected to the emotion and then allowed it room to simply be?

_____

_____

_____

How does it feel to acknowledge and allow the emotion and accompanying sensations without identifying or rejecting?

_____

_____

_____

Unwelcome Emotions

When you find yourself in the grips of an unwelcome emotion, it can seem as though it will last an eternity. Research shows that sadness, often resulting from events such as accidents or loss, can outlast all other emotions in duration—up to 120 hours. The intense emotion of hatred was second in length, dropping to an average of sixty hours, and joy came in third with the potential for thirty-five hours of all-consuming happiness. Yet most emotions move through rather quickly. In fact, the majority of emotions—fear, boredom, anger, greed, shame, jealousy, enthusiasm, and gratitude to name a few—last on average under thirty minutes. (Verduyn and Lavrijsen 2015).

This skewed perception of unwelcome emotions being never-ending and unbearable exists in part because we tend to fight our challenging emotions, judging them and at times ourselves as wrong, unacceptable, and even bad, rather than welcoming them as opportunities for self-engagement and growth. Judging them is turning against yourself. It's a form of self-violence, which only serves to strengthen the rejected parts or feelings. The next time you experience an unwelcome emotion, see if you can view it as an opportunity to get curious.

The exercises that follow will help you accept that there's nothing wrong with you for feeling the way you feel. As you inhabit yourself more fully, you'll begin to consider all of your emotions, even the unwelcome ones, as invaluable messengers. As you learn to make peace with your emotions, you'll learn to tolerate them, knowing that just as sure as they arise, they will leave. As you face each emotion with compassion and understanding, you'll continue to gain greater freedom and peace.

Learning to Listen to the Messages Your Emotions Carry

Your emotions are messengers containing potentially valuable information. The following list sums up the essence of the messages that many of your emotions are trying to convey. It's inspired by my former teacher Bill Bowen.

Fear is about the assessment and preparation to danger.

Anger is all about setting boundaries and asserting needs. In anger, you lose the kind of clarity you need to assert true power.

Rage is a biological defense that arises when your life is threatened. It's trauma-related.

Resentment, when related to trauma, is the awareness that something shouldn't have happened. Grief often underlies resentment.

Disgust tells you there's something figuratively or literally toxic.

Grief is all about opening to loss. Something happened. It's about letting go.

Guilt is the belief *I did something wrong.*

Regret is the belief *I did something wrong, and I'm going to do it differently next time.*

Shame is the belief *I am wrong, and I accept this sentence of my unworthiness. I'm unworthy and unacceptable.*

Jealousy is the belief that *There's not enough love to go around,* and *Life loves others more than me.*

Joy is about opening to the blessings of pleasure and happiness.

Love is about opening to life.

PRACTICE: The Body's Wisdom

This exercise will support you in going inward and listening more closely to the messages your emotions carry. It's good to do when you feel a strong emotion and you're not sure why, you're confused, or you don't know why it keeps showing up.

- Ground and center yourself. Take a few full yet gentle breaths.

- Bring awareness to what emotion is present for you at this time.

- Now drop into your body and notice where you feel the emotion.

- See if you can go right to the center of it. Send the breath to it.

- Ask the emotion, "If you could speak, what would you say? What are you here to tell me?" Don't try to force it. Just let your thoughts recede and see what show's up. You might hear a word, phrase, or sound; see an image in your mind's eye; or feel a sense of knowing or a felt sense. This is you connecting with your inner wisdom.

What message did you receive? If none, try again when you feel safe and focused.

_____

_____

_____

Does this message have meaning to you? Is it something you can act on?

_____

_____

_____

In order to be resilient, you must learn to process, navigate, and tolerate a full range of emotions. We'll explore a few now, beginning with anger and rage.

Anger and Rage

Anger gets your attention. If unchecked, it can be big, loud, fiery, aggressive, and downright frightening. Anger's function is to let you know that something needs to change, and it's anger that can give you the strength and power to create that change. Some degree of anger may surface when feeling frustrated, disappointed, wrongly blamed, harshly judged, ignored, or rejected. Anger is a guide in determining healthy boundaries and advocating for your values and your integrity, and the resulting reorganization can play a role in safeguarding you from becoming a victim.

Since feelings of anger are usually unwelcome, it's an emotion that many girls and some boys learn to suppress (nonexplosive anger tends to be one of the few culturally acceptable emotions for boys and men to express). Similar to how young boys learn to hide their emotions, most young girls are taught to be agreeable and are expected to put their own thoughts and feelings aside if they don't align with the prevailing views. The cost of complying with agreeableness is disempowerment.

You may have grown up in a family that discouraged or flat-out refused to allow the expression of anger. The fear of punishment, withholding of love, shame, and rejection were enough motivation to repress any strong feelings of displeasure and swallow your emotions instead. Repressed, ignored, or denied anger allowed you to be a "good girl or boy," a people pleaser, or a perfectionist. The thing is, repressed and denied anger, like all feelings, eventually finds some form of physical or behavioral expression.

Perhaps you grew up in a very different home, one with someone who had out-of-control, frightening anger. This can leave you highly sensitive and triggered by any sign of anger in another, or you may repeat what was modeled to you with explosive outbursts of your own. In either case, you're left with the negative impact of unexpressed or overexpressed anger on your health and relationships.

How was the expression of anger modeled to you as a child?

_____

_____

_____

Do you struggle with feeling or expressing anger now (too much or not at all)?

_____

_____

_____

Do you ever feel as though you're holding onto anger?

_____

_____

_____

Anger invites us to go deeper, to bring awareness to the underlying feelings crying out for recognition and acceptance. There are often feelings of fear, grief, or shame stemming from hurt, rejection from others or from oneself, and loss of love lying deep below the anger. If we identify what feeling is present under anger's guise, we can ask ourselves what need is not being met. It's our unmet needs that drive our anger.

Anger's often heightened by a trigger connecting it to something painful from your past, which in turn amplifies its intensity. It's essential to separate the past hurt from the present upset so you respond in a way that's proportionate to the current situation and avoid taking out the full force of your anger on someone undeserving of it.

While acknowledging and accepting feelings of anger is important, holding on to anger is more harmful than helpful. When you begin to get angry, a series of biological responses designed to help you respond to the stressor are activated, setting off a chain reaction of the hormones cortisol, adrenaline, and noradrenaline. You need these hormones in healthy doses, but too much becomes toxic for your body.

Excess cortisol can lead to a loss of neurons in two regions of your brain: the prefrontal cortex, which can prevent you from using good judgment, and the hippocampus, which can weaken your short-term memory and prevent the proper formation of new memories. Excess cortisol can also decrease serotonin, the feel-good hormone, making it easier to feel anger, depression, and physical pain. Stress hormones can negatively impact your immune, thyroid, digestive, and cardiovascular health as well. Holding onto anger can be more destructive to you than to the target of your rage.

Anger needs to be acknowledged and to find expression. You want to become aware of how you can let that energy flow through you so it's released on a molecular level. As you grow mindful of how you meet and give expression to this intense feeling, you'll no longer reject or fear your anger. As you become viscerally aware of your anger through the practices that follow, you'll strengthen your capacity for healthy assertiveness and agency.

— *Story:* I Don't Get Angry

While discussing anger in a survivor's group I facilitate, several members shared they were struggling with frequent feelings of rage in relation to having been sexually assaulted. Then one member, Erin, quietly said that she doesn't get angry. On further exploration, it seemed to be a point of pride. I often see this early on in working with clients: a firm belief that it's not acceptable to get angry. Therefore, feelings of anger aren't acknowledged, and they're pushed away or denied. While it may seem like a good thing to avoid any and all conflict, it's not so good for your health and well-being. Studies show that suppressing anger can eventually lead to diseases such as cancer (Thomas et al. 2000).

I knew Erin was angry with the men who assaulted her, but it was still too hard for her to go against what she'd been taught—that being angry was not acceptable. As a young girl, she learned her lesson well, to be agreeable, but this lesson was not serving her in her healing.

It took time for Erin to give herself permission to process the anger. As Erin gradually started listening to her emotions, becoming mindful of the sensations she was experiencing, she learned to acknowledge, allow, and accept the anger, to tolerate it, and when called for, to give it healthy expression. It never got big and explosive, which she'd feared. Learning to process anger was an important part of her healing, and in time Erin transformed her anger from what had been debilitating into self-agency and liberation.

— Story: I'm Angry All the Time

Frequent feelings and unintentional expressions of anger and rage were the primary symptoms that lead Di to seek help with healing from molestation. Di and her partner argued often, and although they loved each other deeply, they were on the verge of splitting up. Her dramatic outbursts of anger would routinely lead to feelings of self-loathing. She realized this level of emotion was negatively impacting all of her relationships, and she was worried she was pushing everyone she cared about away, especially her partner.

When I first showed Di some ways to give her anger expression, such as the "Shifting the Anger—Whoosh" practice (below), she was resistant and dismissive. Several weeks passed without much improvement in the frequency and intensity of her conflicts until one day she surprised me, saying with a smile, "That whoosh thing really works." She'd gotten into another argument with her partner, only this time she remembered "Shifting the Anger." Di told her partner she was going outside for a few minutes to calm herself. This gave Di time and space to attend to herself as she supported her nervous system's move back toward calm and safety. After five or so minutes, Di was able to go back inside and continue the discussion with her partner from a place of connection that lead to deeper understanding and repair.

As Di and I looked at the events that lead to her episodes of anger, she began to realize much of the anger directed at her partner had little to do with them. Di started to work through anger from the past and learned to communicate her needs before feeling angry by making requests. Eventually her relationship to anger transformed to healthy expression of anger, strengthened communication skills, and clearer boundaries. Di's relationship with her partner was transformed as well. They got engaged a few months later.

Exploring Safe Forms of Expression, Giving Shape to the Anger

Your muscles enable all bodily systems to function, respond to, and absorb mental and emotional strain. Without adequate relaxation following highly stressful states, such as anger, tension collects generating deeper, longer-lasting harm. Over time your muscles can become organized in this restricted form, holding emotions and trauma. The now-frozen anger, fear, or grief can build a fearful or depressive attitude into your physical structure, which in turn continues to enable the mental state. To alter these patterns and heal any wounds, it's necessary to work with both the physical and the psychological structuring of anger.

The next time you're feeling anger, stress, upset, or frustration, notice: Does your body want you to move? If so, trust your body and follow its lead. Is there an impulse to push, throw, punch, or kick? Your body may be trying to release some negative or stuck energy.

PRACTICE: Anger Strategies

Try one of the following when angry, being sure not to hurt yourself or anyone else. Downloadable copy of this practice at http://newharbinger.com/46509.

- Do the "Shifting the Anger—Whoosh" practice (below).

- Push against a sturdy wall by placing your hands on the wall and your feet several feet away so your body is at an angle. Feel the strength of your spine as you push as hard as you can.

- Throw pillows or bean bags.

- Punch the back of a couch, bed, or a punching bag.

- Kick a couch, pillow, ball, or sand.

- Hold one end of a towel in each hand then twist with all of your strength.

- Stomp your feet.

- Go for a walk, run, or dance out the anger.

- Do the "Fists to Palms and Willing Hands" practice (below).

Do you want to give voice to your anger or frustration?

- Make the sound of the anger as you exhale a full breath.

- Yell into a pillow or outside in nature.

- Sing out whatever your anger wants to say.

Journal or reflect on what your anger or frustration is trying to tell you.

- Are your feelings a response to your internal voice, or are they a response to something or someone outside of you?

- Has a boundary been crossed or violated, or are you having a hard time making one?

- Locate where the anger lives in your body, and then ask if it has a message and what it needs to feel better.

- Is this need something you can offer yourself, such as giving yourself compassion, going for a walk, or offering forgiveness, or is this a request you would like to make of another, such as for a hug, for a boundary, or to listen empathically?

When you're done processing your feelings, give yourself thanks for the courage you showed in facing your anger, upset, or frustration head on. As you become viscerally aware of your anger, you'll strengthen your capacity for healthy assertiveness and agency. Next time you feel the heat of anger, try welcoming it with curiosity. See if you can make it your ally. Lots of information is alive in it.

PRACTICE: Fists to Palms and Willing Hands

This is a very subtle practice to help shift feelings of anger, upset, overwhelm, or frustration.

- Take a moment to scan your body. Notice what you're sensing and feeling. How intense is the emotion?

- Extend your arms out in front of you, parallel to the ground, hands facing down.

- Make fists with both hands.

- Now intensify your fists.

- Intensify your grip even more.

- Turn your arms over so your fists are now facing upward, intensify again.

- Now slowly, as in super slow motion, open your hands.

What do you notice after this exercise? Do you feel any shift in how you're feeling?

_____

_____

Do you feel a sense of release, perhaps letting go?

_____

_____

Even a slight shift is one step closer toward ventral vagal safety and calm, and movement in that direction is exactly what you're looking for.

Willing hands is a practice I learned by way of Dr. Joan Borysenko, who said its origins lie in a spiritual tradition. I shared this with a minister, and after trying it, she exclaimed with a smile, "Oh, of course, I do this all day long!" It's helpful when you need to temper or contain your anger around others, for example at school or work. Simply place your hands on your lap, palms open and facing up, or, when standing by your sides, palms facing outward. This receptive hand position makes it hard to communicate in anger.

PRACTICE: Shifting the Anger—Whoosh

This is my favorite practice for generating movement toward ventral vagal calm when angry, upset, overwhelmed, or frustrated. It's inspired by Donna Eden (2012), an expert in the field of Energy Medicine. In addition to releasing the energies of these emotions, it's an effective way to let go of stress. Download the instructions at http://newharbinger.com/46509.

The movement in the first part is meant to be done fairly quickly, within one breath cycle. Try walking through the first five prompts to get the hang of it, and then find the rhythm of your breath.

- Begin standing. Rate the intensity of the emotion you're feeling on a scale of 1 to 10.

- On the inhale, raise your arms out in front of you, elbows slightly bent, hands facing one another. Make fists.

- Continuing to inhale, in a sweeping motion, swing your arms and fists down to your sides, then behind you, continuing up and over your head.

- With hands still facing each other, reach way up as you release your fists.

- Relax your knees, letting them bend slightly as you drop your arms down the front of your body, hands cutting through the air as you exhale. Make the sound _whoosh_, or any other powerful sound that arises from within, giving the emotion expression.

- Repeat the whole process three or more times. On the final repetition, exhale fully as you slowly bring your arms down.

- Brush off any residual feelings of anger with a sweeping motion of your hands down your arms, torso, and legs. Shake it off. Direct the energy into the ground to be recycled and used at a later time for something good.

- Take a few deep breaths, then scan your body, and notice what sensations and feelings are present. On a scale of 1 to 10, how would you rate the intensity of the emotion?

If it's 5 or above: Notice if the feelings lessened. Even if you move down only one or two points, that's still a shift of your nervous system toward calm. Check in with yourself and see what's needed now. You might want to journal your unedited thoughts to give further expression to the anger.

If your number is under 5, or you're no longer feeling anger, stress, upset, or frustration, continue with these steps:

- Raise your arms out to your sides, palms facing up. Now think of what qualities you'd like to attract to yourself at this time, for example a sense of ease, calm, and connection.

- Sense into these qualities until you feel them resonating throughout your body.

- Swoop them up with your hands to your heart center, staying there for several more breaths as you absorb this energy.

Reflecting on Anger

By now you know that anger needs expression. At the same time, you don't want to allow your anger to dictate your reactions and your choices. It's important to take responsibility for your anger, to speak of it when possible rather than from it, to work with it, to give it healthy expression, and then to let it go. Once you've cooled down from an episode of anger, ask yourself the following questions.

Did the anger feel more like energy or muscle tension, and did it want to do something?

_____

_____

What did you do to help give the anger expression?

_____

_____

Was the intensity of your anger proportionate to whomever or whatever you were angry at?

_____

_____

Were you triggered by past hurts?

_____

_____

Did any good came out of your expression of anger, for example the realization that you needed to set a boundary or make a request?

_____

_____

Do you think you could have expressed your feelings of anger in a healthier way?

_____

_____

What might you do differently in the future?

_____

_____

Give yourself thanks for the courage you showed in facing your anger and other challenging emotions head on. With practice, expressing and managing your anger will pay off with improved relationships, health, and well-being.

Resentment

At some point in your healing, you'll likely experience feelings of resentment. It's natural to feel resentment for an injustice. Resentment's an acknowledgment that whatever happened shouldn't have happened to you. Resentment and revenge fantasies can feel empowering in comparison to feelings of powerlessness and internalized shame. There's a lot more energy in resentment. At its best, resentment's a sign that you value yourself, a healthy reaction to unhealthy circumstances.

In terms of your nervous system, resentment related to the assault(s) can be seen as anger that's waiting to mobilize a fight response that was never able to be completed. Your body had to override its instinct to fight in order to keep you alive (freeze, the shock of betrayal), or if you didn't freeze, you were rendered powerless (by threat, by physical force, or were drugged), all of which prevent the fight response from coming to completion.

Resentment motivates you to action, but when there's no action to take, resentment can take hold of the body-mind. If unchecked, it becomes chronic, sending your nervous system into hyper-arousal. Thinking becomes black-and-white, focusing on the negative, and everything and everyone can look like a threat. You've been through a lot and have good reason for the resentment, and at the same time you don't deserve to live in a chronic state of resentment keeping you perpetually tied to the trauma(s).

If resentment's been ongoing, what do you think it does for you?

_____

_____

_____

How does your body experience resentment? For example, do your shoulders feel tight, or are your hands tense?

_____

_____

_____

What is it costing you?

_____

_____

_____

What do you imagine will happen if you relax the resentment?

_____

_____

_____

What might you do to shift your relationship to the resentment?

_____

_____

_____

Here are a few things you might try:

- Use the anger exercises in this chapter as needed.

- Try replacing resentment for shame in the "Sending Back the Shame" practice at the end of this chapter.

- Put your unedited feelings down on paper.

- Speak publicly about sexual assault. RAINN has a program called the RAINN Speakers Bureau.

- If you're comfortable with it, share your story on a blog, podcast, or social media.

- Organize a survivors' group or join an online community, such as http://weareher.com and http://malesurvivors.org.

- Get involved with organizations that support change, such as http://metoomvmt.org, http://survivorsknow.org, http://weareultraviolet.org, http://survivorsagenda.org, http://generationfive.org, and http://rainn.org.

Resentment's a good reminder to practice self-compassion, to treat yourself the way you want others to treat you, and to express gratitude for those who treat you with kindness and respect. Grief, the focus of chapter 8, is often found underlying resentment. Now, we'll take a look at another challenging emotion, shame.

Shame

Shame is one of, if not the most, intensely painful emotions. The feeling that you're flawed and therefore unworthy of love and belonging takes hold of your body and mind, denying your basic nature, which is fundamentally good. Shame's tricky because it can hide beneath anger, fear, or other emotions, making it hard to detect. It causes you to hide, constrict, or pull away, cutting you off from the safe social connection that's vital in healing from trauma. If unchecked, shame becomes chronic and, as with anger, can negatively impact your health. Just as with other emotions, developing an awareness and tolerance helps ease the distress caused by the collapse of shame.

Like fight, flight, and freeze, shame is a survival response that may have protected you from something even more painful. Shame functions as a signal of interpersonal or social danger and can serve as a defensive strategy to interpersonal conflict and threat. When you're shamed, you can feel like you don't belong and it's not safe. Therefore, shame is accompanied by fear. Whereas fear focuses on the source of threat, as in someone or something is not safe, shame feels personal, such as not feeling seen, recognized, respected, rejected, abandoned, defective, chronically unloved, unlovable, or without value.

Do any of these feel familiar to you?

_____

_____

_____

Feelings of shame are rooted in childhood, experienced as early as fifteen months of age as a somatic sensation of I feel bad. Parents need some way of teaching children what's safe and acceptable and what's not. Feelings of shame help inhibit potentially harmful behaviors. When a child wants to touch a hot stove or run into the street, the parent will yell, "No!" The young child, feeling the overwhelm of disappointing their parent, may drop their head and begin to cry. If the parent isn't attuned to the child's needs, comforting and letting them know it was their action not them that was wrong, that they are loved, then shame takes hold.

Shame is also rooted in trauma. An infant who experiences trauma can't comprehend that they're a good person in a bad situation and instead internalize that they themselves are bad. This becomes a deep-rooted belief that something is wrong with them, that they're unworthy of love or fundamentally flawed. And shame has the potential of being life-threatening. If you're expelled from the tribe (family, community) before age ten, it can be deadly since a child's not capable of surviving on their own.

What is your earliest memory of shame?

_____

_____

_____

Was there any repair or any reassurance that you are good and loved from an adult? If not, what words did you need to hear?

_____

_____

_____

How do you think this experience has impacted you?

_____

_____

_____

Shame's not only triggered by failures, criticisms, and harsh judgements. It can also be triggered by successes, such as feeling proud and being seen. What shame desperately needs is:

- mindful, somatic, and cognitive acknowledgement that shame is present

- not viewing shame as a reflection of who you are

- an understanding that shame is an active and protective survival resource

- kindness, acceptance, and love (from you).

Although compassion from others doesn't tend to help with shame, when you experience shame, bring in the "Self-Compassion Steps" (chapter 2). The exercises that follow offer more skills you can use to process this painful and immobilizing emotion.

Fawning

Some survivors have deep feelings of shame for having become unexplainably agreeable during or after the traumatic experience. This is the survival strategy known as fawning, where one displays exaggerated affection, flattery, and adoration to try to curry favor. While processing and healing from two sexual assaults, biologist and author Rebecca Heiss, PhD, (2019) wondered why she had sought to appease an assailant by moaning. She began researching the question and soon realized an impulse to appease the perpetrator may be built into our biology.

Submission can be an active defense when fight or flight is too dangerous or impossible. Heiss (2019) explains, "Our closest primate cousins, bonobos and chimpanzees, bare their teeth in a grimace remarkably similar to the human smile when they are afraid and hope to ward of an attack" (43). She went on to say, "Men who are rejected can move swiftly toward violence, so responding passively and even smiling may save lives or, at least, prevent [further] injury. We may be genetically programed to literally grin and bear it" (43).

This illustrates once again that how you responded in the face of trauma didn't have intentionality to it. As neuroception sent your nervous system into the fight-flight-freeze response, your perception and decision making were no longer available. Being sexually abused is not something you did; it's something that was done to you. Whatever you felt and however you responded wasn't your fault. It's time to begin honoring yourself as courageous and your body as heroic for having done what it needed to do to survive.

Shame vs. Guilt

Survivors will often share their feelings of guilt for having been sexually assaulted or for some aspect of the traumatic event. On further exploration, they usually come to the realization that what they're feeling is not guilt; rather it's the intense pain of shame. One way to distinguish the two is guilt tells you that *you've done something wrong*, that you likely went against your values, while shame tells you that *you are wrong*. Shame is the belief that you are fundamentally flawed or unworthy.

Guilt	Shame
I did something wrong.	I am wrong.
The focus is on the behavior.	The focus is on the self.
You experience psychological discomfort.	You experience intense pain.
You may feel tension, regret, or remorse.	You may feel small, worthless, or powerless.
You may have broken your moral standards.	You may see yourself as unworthy, defective.
You may be concerned with your effect on others.	You may be concerned with others' evaluations of you.
You may want to confess, apologize, or repair.	You may want to hide, escape, or retaliate.
Irrational guilt can lead to self-punishment over behavior change, causing more guilt.	Unprocessed shame can lead to disconnection from others, depression, and substance abuse.
Healthy guilt allows you to right a wrong, do better next time, and forgive yourself, and can lead to healing.	Processed shame can lead to self-acceptance, connection, a sense of belonging, and healing.

It does not matter if you flirted with them, what you were wearing, if you were drunk or high, if you let them touch you, if you were too young to know that what they did was wrong, if you didn't tell, if your body felt aroused, if you didn't yell for help, if you didn't fight… It doesn't matter. You're not guilty for what was done to you without your consent or when you were too young to give consent. What happened to you was truly beyond your control. It was not your fault, and you are not guilty, yet it's up to you to begin altering your relationship to it.

Shame and Your Inner Critic

The cognitive aspect of shame shows up with the inner critic. Like shame, the critic developed when you were very young, roughly two to five years old, as you learned to control impulses, such as when to reach for that cookie. Freud referred to this part of the mind as the super-ego, which reflects the internalization of cultural norms and punishes misbehavior with feelings of guilt or shame. This is inner self-regulation, a necessary part of development, yet shameful childhood feelings without repair create a powerful inner critic.

Children take on or assimilate critical and negative emotions parents or primary caregivers experience, especially when directed at the child. In this sense, the parent's inner critic is passed on, and children learn to parent themselves in much the same way they were parented.

There are two things necessary to weaken the inner critic's impact. You need to learn to disidentify from the critic's negative messages and to accept this part of yourself, to make friends. As you do so, the attacks will soften and grow less frequent.

To befriend the critic, it's helpful to understand that its constant judgments and discouraging negative messages about your self-worth are really distorted attempts to protect you from failure and humiliation. Your inner critic is still very young, and in a sense, it's stuck in a time warp, continuing to discourage and berate you in an often-misguided attempt to protect you. If you reject it as a part of yourself, it strengthens. Once you accept that your inner critic developed out of necessity with the honorable goal of protecting you, you can begin to meet its voice with compassion.

PRACTICE: Distancing and Befriending Your Inner Critic

1. Recognizing that you're in the process of self-attack is the first step in befriending your inner critic. It's easy to identify by the way it devalues you, always putting you down or making you feel bad in some way. The next time you hear the critic, pause to really listen. Notice if the voice, the tone, or the phrasing sounds like a parent, a caregiver, teacher, coach, or older sibling. Some individuals can identify a source; for others, it's many voices combined.

What does your inner critic say?

_____

_____

_____

Can you identify the voice or voices of your inner critic?

_____

2. Communicate with the inner critic. Thank it for showing up to try to protect you, and tell it, "You're doing the best you can," "You've got this," or "You're just fine the way you are." These new words and phrases will have a different impact on your somatic experience. Be sure to use a soft or calming tone.

What are some phrases that might help calm your inner critic?

_____

_____

Sense where the critic resides in your body. Where is it located?

_____

3. Ask it to move further away, to speak, for example, from your little toe. This is a distancing technique from Michael Yapko, PhD. Another is to pick your favorite cartoon character. If you don't have one, speak aloud in a funny voice the words your critic is saying. Even better, look in a mirror while doing so. These are silly, but they work!

As you learn to acknowledge, accept, and disidentify with your inner critic, it will diminish. Its attacks will no longer have the same hold on you.

Silence and Shame

Those born with male gender assigned to them are socialized to be strong, to not be victims. Boys and men who have been sexually assaulted have the burden of overcoming the expectation that they're supposed to be able to protect themselves. To not do so can wrongly draw into question their masculinity. As a result, many males remain silent, minimizing or denying sexual abuse all together.

Perpetrators, especially those who molest children, use shame as a weapon to silence their victims. This can range from telling the victim it's their special secret; accusing the victim of wanting or asking for it; telling the victim they're unworthy, unwanted, or dirty; and gaslighting. If a relationship of dominance and subordination played out, feelings of humiliation, degradation, and shame are often part of the survivor's experience.

Many survivors feel shame simply because it happened to them, as though they're somehow responsible or tainted as a result. The thing is, shame doesn't belong to the victim; it belongs to the one who committed the shameful and despicable act. They're the one who deserves to carry the burden and pain of shame. When asked her intention in writing *Know My Name*, Chanel Miller shared, "To be free from that shame that was never ours to carry in the first place, and to say by the end, 'I'm going to put this down now, it's your turn to carry it, it's not mine anymore'" (OWN 2019).

Your Body's Relation to Shame

Shame is active and protective. Most physical signals of shame appear submissive, designed to escape conflict, deescalate, or limit damage. Shame can show up in your body as signs of discomfort and agitation, nervous laughter, downcast eyes, gaze aversion, flushing, face touching, and lip manipulation. You might experience a sinking feeling in your stomach, head, or shoulders; feel your chest dropping in a slumped posture or an overall sense of collapse; wanting to curl up or turn away; or a loss of energy.

We avoid shame whenever possible, but it catches us off guard. You might notice, from the nervous system's perspective, at first you feel a sense of shock, which can be accompanied by flushing. You may have a hard time finding your words or being able to speak, along with an impulse to turn away or disappear. Next comes a low arousal depressed or freeze state, the painful collapse of dorsal vagal narrowing your view of yourself, others, and the world.

The collapsed physical posture of shame reinforces shamed-based cognitions, just as the thoughts you have and the words you use evoke bodily responses. These powerful bodily responses of shame accompanied by a skewed perspective exacerbate the somatic responses and create a vicious cycle of shame.

PRACTICE: Somatically Exploring Shame

The following exercise will help you better understand how shame shapes you and how to find self-agency through postural changes when in the grips of shame. If you feel the need, stop and return to "Coming into Safety" (chapter 1) or find your object of safety (chapter 3).

The next time you feel shame coming on:

- acknowledge that shame is present

- shift your focus away from your shame-based words, thoughts, and emotions

- focus on your bodily sensations

How does shame show up in your body? Do you feel your stomach sinking, do you look down or away, or do you want to curl up and disappear?

_____

_____

_____

How does this posture support you?

_____

_____

_____

Do you think this posture could be a hinderance in any way?

_____

_____

_____

Now, shift your bodily posture. Try experimenting, be gentle and go slow. If it feels like too much, you can move back into the posture you began with. Some postural changes that help reduce or alleviate shame, depression, and numbing are:

- grounding through the bottoms of your feet

- lengthening your spine by increasing space between the vertebrae in the lower to middle back

- slowly lifting and moving your shoulders back

- gradually lifting your chin and head

- gently bringing your gaze up and focusing on something at eye level

After trying this exercise, notice how you feel. Are you less fearful, a little calmer, or a little more confident?

_____

_____

Simply naming what you're feeling or experiencing can help you be the observer of it rather than identifying as it. To become more aware of your shame response, download the "Shame Questions" from http://newharbinger.com/46509.

⌐ *Story:* A Gray Filter of Shame

Aria was molested by her grandfather as a young child over a period of several years. He told her that he loved her, that she was very special, and that it was their secret. Like many molestation victims, she was too young to understand what he was doing to her. As Aria got older, she began to somatically sense how wrong his actions were. She felt an icky feeling in her mouth and throughout her body. Around the time she reached puberty, a deep sense of shame surfaced for how she'd learned about sex and how her body had responded.

Just as you have no control over how your nervous system will respond to a threat, you have no control over how your body's biological arousal response will react to intimate touch, even when it's uninvited and unwanted. If you've never felt unwanted arousal, it feels awful, like your body's betraying you.

When I explained to Aria that she couldn't have controlled her body's biological reactions, that many molestation victims feel like their body betrayed them, she responded, "I never thought about it as my body betraying me. I thought of it as my soul." Hearing that Aria believed her soul had betrayed her was heartbreaking and lead to further processing of how this deep betrayal manifested in her body.

She tearfully shared that for most of her life, up until recently, anytime she experienced feelings of pleasure, a gray filter would fall over everything, preventing her from enjoying anything fully. This had made her question if it was all worth it. Lately, while doing some of the various activities she enjoys, she no longer felt that filter of dullness. Instead she'd begun to experience a warm feeling in her chest that radiated outward. When I asked if she thought the gray filter might be shame, Aria said that she'd never thought of it as shame, "But it makes sense." A few weeks later she shared that she could finally identify what had been haunting her and read a powerfully expressive and insightful poem she'd written directed at the gray fog. Now that the shame could be seen clearly in the light of day, it was finally losing the grip it had held on her for all those years.

— *Story:* Is There Something Wrong with Me?

When Sean was a boy, his mother would bring him into her room for long periods of time while she dressed. He would sit at the foot of her bed while she put on her stockings and heels and made herself up, all while confiding in him as though he were her friend. When he was about seven, his father put an abrupt end to his wife's inappropriate behavior by banning Sean from their bedroom. As Sean hit puberty, he began to fetishize women's feet and high-heel shoes, a fetish that at times led to actions that later brought on feelings of shame. Years later when he came to see me, he was having implicit memories of his mother molesting him. As Sean told me his story, his shoulders slouched forward, he asked from a deep place of shame if something was wrong with him.

As Sean and I unpacked shame and anger in relation to his mother's sexual abuse, a new memory surfaced, one he'd never shared before. He had been sexually assaulted by an older boy in the shower at camp. Rage accompanied this memory as he recalled the pain and confusion the assault had caused him. Back when the assault happened, it had brought into question his sexual orientation. Confusion for both male and female survivors can arise around sexual orientation depending on the gender of the perpetrator. An example is a boy who's gay and is molested by a man might conclude that he wouldn't be into men if he hadn't been molested, leading him to deny a part of his identity. He may avoid relationships with men altogether causing much pain in the long run.

In Sean's case, at the time of the assault, he wondered if it meant he was gay, even though he was interested in girls. It had been many years since he'd thought of or questioned this; all that was left now was the rage. I asked Sean what impulse his body had as he felt into the anger. He motioned his arm as though he were hitting or stabbing something. I invited him to stand and put his whole body into the movement. He threw himself into this expression until the urge began to subside and a release of emotion followed. Through safely sharing what he had kept secret and somatically completing what his body could not do at the time of the assault, Sean was able to unburden himself of the devastating anger and shame.

PRACTICE: Sending Back the Shame

For this exercise, it's helpful to have the support of a therapist. It can be done on your own, but either way, do not do it until you've done the previous exercises in this book. If you get triggered, you can stop at any time and do "Coming into Safety" (chapter 1). Find a quiet place to reflect where you feel safe. Take some time to ground and center yourself.

- Notice where the shame is located in your body. Does it have a shape, a color, a texture, or any other characteristics?

- Place your hand where it's located and send your breath to it.

- Ask the shame, "If you had a voice, what sound would you make?" On your next full exhalation, give yourself permission to make the sound, as loud as you want and as many times as your body needs. You can make the sound into a pillow if you're worried about others hearing.

- Next notice if the shame wants to move. If so, you can assist it in moving out of you. It might want to come up and out or down through your legs and out. You might imagine reaching into your body and pulling it out and reaching back for more. Let your inner knowing lead you, taking as long as you need.

- Once it feels like all of it's out, brush and shake it off your arms, legs, and torso, in big sweeping motions. Direct it into the ground where the energy can be recycled into something good.

- Now imagine, if you could send the perpetrator anywhere in the universe, where would that be? Some survivors choose a place on Earth; some put them in a cage or bury them; some put them in a rocket ship and blast them into outer space. It can be as far away as you want; anywhere is possible as long as its somewhere that helps you feel safe.

- Connect with the image of sending them far away. Watch them get smaller and smaller. This is the image you'll think of whenever you remember them—tiny, impotent, and far, far away.

- Notice if there's anything you want to say to them. If so, say it now. Yell if you want to.

- If you feel the need, brush off the energy and direct it into the ground. Take a moment to honor whatever emotions are arising. Is there anything you're needing?

You may feel exhausted or emotionally drained after doing this practice, so be gentle and offer gratitude and appreciation to yourself. You might journal, light a candle, burn sage, or diffuse some essential oils. A warm cup of tea and a relaxing bath may feel comforting. Notice what your body-mind is needing and honor it.

Again, it's important not to judge your feelings. Judging them is turning against yourself. It's a form of self-violence that only serves to strengthen the rejected parts or feelings. Treat yourself with tenderness and care. Appreciate yourself, your courage and strength, for having taken the time to explore how painful and often-debilitating emotions show up in you.

CHAPTER 8

Grief for All You've Lost and Reclaiming Your Sexual Power

It's inevitable that at some point in your healing journey grief will visit. It usually shows up after you've made some progress, after a deep revelation or a new understanding of how the sexual assault(s) have impacted you; of your decisions and opportunities; and of your connection to vitality, intimacy, others, community, and life. One of the things you're likely to grieve most while healing is the way the traumatic event has impacted your sexuality, including how you intimately relate to yourself and to a partner(s); discomfort with touch; triggers, dissociation, or flashbacks during sex; and sexual aversion or sexual compulsion. If your health has suffered, this will also be a part of the grieving process and why we'll look at trauma, inflammation, and the vagus nerve.

Survivors of molestation often feel a profound sense of grief for the innocence they were robbed of. Adult survivors can feel grief over a loss of trust they once had in others or with how memories of their former free-spirited self have been replaced with feelings of cynicism and jadedness. This kind of grief is called ambiguous grief because it's less tangible than the loss of a loved one, yet just as with any other grief, the weight of ambiguous grief can feel unbearable.

Grief is a process of letting go, of discovery, and of healing. Like trauma, you cannot release grief with your thoughts alone, as Carol Staudacher (1994) wrote, "The brain must follow the heart at a respectful distance" (7). Unresolved grief expends considerable amounts of energy. The only way to heal from grief is through. When tended to, grief will gradually diminish.

Grief involves pain. Physical and emotional pain operate identically in the brain and are inextricably linked. Ongoing pain always contains an emotional component, some sensation, or physical pain, along with thoughts or beliefs, such as a sense of loneliness or fear of what the future holds. These thoughts often block recovery or contribute to the cycle of pain.

As with flashbacks, to ease the pain cycle:

- move from identifying with the pain—*I am the pain,* or *I am the suffering,* to *I am experiencing the suffering*

- observe and detach from the pain—*I am experiencing the sensations that are underneath the pain*

When you recoil from the sensations, they become a source of even more suffering (Levine and Phillips 2012).

You cannot experience profound well-being without acceptance of, rather than pushing against, the tough, sometimes sorrowful reality of life. When we face our vulnerability and helplessness directly, letting the feelings arise, build in intensity, and then fade away, we begin to experience the rawness of the emotion without identifying with it. When you stop resisting and avoiding the ever-changing quality of life, you relax and become available to the present.

Resistance Breath

Resistance breath can help you be present with what is. Resistance breathing is any type of breathing that slows the flow of air, such as pursing your lips, placing your tongue against the inside of your upper teeth, breathing through a straw, humming, singing, or chanting. Another example is a cat's calming purr. Resistance breathing creates a vibrational sound and slightly increases the pressure in your lungs, stimulating your parasympathetic nervous system, which is soothing and supports a calming ventral vagal state.

Taking slower and deeper breaths promotes lung health and greater oxygenation. You can change the messages being sent from the body's respiratory system to the brain—impacting major brain centers involved in thought, emotion, and behavior—simply by changing the rate, depth, and pattern of your breathing (Brown and Gerbarg 2012). Taking the time to slowly and rhythmically hum on your exhalation is a wonderful resistance breath practice.

PRACTICE: Resistance Breath and Vocalizing

Grief is a movement of energy associated with loss, and like anger, it needs expression. Crying is form of expression. We can have a big messy cry that facilitates a sense of release, but we can also get caught in a state of flooding that doesn't bring any comfort. This practice can help you give expression to the sound of your grief, which may or may not be the sound of crying. I encourage you to try it with other emotions as well.

- Lying down on a mat or other comfortable surface, close or bring your eyes to a soft focus. Feel the Earth supporting you. Relax your face, jaw, neck, shoulders, and hands.

- Bring awareness to your breath. Breathe slowly and gently in through your nose and out through pursed lips for several minutes.

- Do you feel grief, or is there another emotion present?

- Where do you feel this emotion in your body? Feel into the sensation that correlates with the emotion. If you can't find it, ask yourself, "How is my body telling me that I feel this emotion?"

- Place one or both hands on the surface of your skin above the sensation.

- What sound does this sensation want to express? With no judgments, no sense of right or wrong, give expression to what arises. Let this sound be present throughout the out-breath.

- Repeat the sound several times as loud as you're comfortable with, until it feels complete.

- Breathe slowly and gently in through your nose and out through pursed lips for a few minutes.

- Notice how your body-mind feels. Has the sensation or the emotion changed?

_____

_____

_____

For help processing unresolved grief, try the "Grief Resolution Letter," available for download at http://newharbinger.com/46509.

PRACTICE: **Energy Shift**

Grief can make it hard to connect with your vitality. This exercise can create a shift. Even a small shift of energy is a move in the right direction.

- Begin standing. Take note of how much vitality you're feeling. Inhale as you raise your arms up above you. Imagine that you're drawing in energy from above you as it enters through your crown chakra (located at the top or crown of your head).

- Bring your hands to your heart on the exhale.

- Inhaling, bend your knees and reach down to the ground. Imagine you are drawing in energy from the Earth.

- On the exhale, bring your hands back to your heart.

- Repeat several times.

- Do you notice a shift in your energy?

While giving grief expression helps move the energy through you, grief cannot be rushed. It leaves when it is ready. Once you've had the time and space to process much of your grief, you might ask, "Is there something that wants to be born out of the loss?"

Sexual Aversion

The impact trauma has on a survivor's sexuality can bring about tremendous grief. Understanding why your body-mind is responding the way it is can help with healing and processing any related suffering. Unintegrated trauma can lead to difficulties with physical intimacy due to the nervous system's tendency to remain in a sympathetic high alert state in an attempt to protect the body. This state can be elevated by sexual arousal, triggering trauma associations that have the capacity to mentally fuse sex with sexual abuse (Rellini and Meston 2006). So, it's not uncommon for survivors go through a period of sexual aversion, also known as sexual anorexia, or the opposite extreme, sexual compulsion. Some survivors move from one into the other prior to or during their healing.

The trauma inflicted by sexual assault causes many survivors to shut down their sexuality in an attempt to avoid feelings of fear, betrayal, and shame. Emily Nagoski (2015) explains, "Sensations, contexts, and ideas that used to be interpreted as sexually relevant may instead now be interpreted by your brain as threats so that sexy contexts actually hit the brakes" (127). Unconsciously turning off desire, numbing the pelvic floor, or dissociating to avoid having to deal with the trauma's painful triggers and flashbacks are all signs of aversion. Obsessing about not having sex or believing that your appearance is the reason you were assaulted (research shows motives are varied and difficult to quantify) can also be signs. Some female-bodied survivors experience vaginismus, painful constriction of the muscles of the vagina, that can lead to aversion due to extreme physical discomfort (see the section "Sexual Trauma and Issues with the Pelvic Floor" below). Male-bodied survivors who experience erectile dysfunction can also become adverse.

Stress plays a role as you're more likely to interpret all stimuli as threats when stressed (worry, anxiety, fear, terror, anger, frustration, irritation, and rage). When stressed-out, your nervous system can move into a sympathetic or dorsal vagal state as blood rushes away from the prefrontal cortex, digestive, and reproductive organs, prioritizing survival needs. For the majority of survivors, stress turns off arousal, blocking sexual pleasure. Nagoski (2015) explains that healing "requires an environment of relative security and the ability to separate the physiology of freeze from the experience of fear" (125) so the panic and rage that couldn't find their way to the surface in the aftermath of the trauma "can discharge, completing their cycles at last" (126; as in chapter 7, "Sending Back the Shame"). Physical activity, sleep, affection, meditation, mindfulness, yoga, tai chi, body scans, vocalizing, creative expression, and body self-care are all effective in "completing the stress response cycle and recalibrating your central nervous system into a calm state" (122).

Have you avoided sex since the trauma took place, since your body began to thaw, or while you've been working to heal? If so, was this a conscious choice?

_____

_____

Can you think of any ways that aversion has helped you?

_____

_____

_____

What do you associate with sex, both positive and negative?

_____

_____

_____

Are these associations based on consensual sex or nonconsensual sex?

_____

_____

Avoiding sex may help you feel and stay safe for a time. For some, taking an intentional break from sex during recovery can promote healing. The thing is, ongoing aversion comes at a cost: reinforcing fear, robbing you of deep connection and intimacy with yourself and others, and the full range of the human experience.

Another aspect to consider when looking at aversion, especially for survivors in long-term relationships, is that unlike in the movies, sexual desire's not always spontaneous, nor is spontaneous desire necessary to become aroused. Responsive sexual desire happens when there's a willingness to engage in sex even when desire or arousal is not initially present. With the right sexual stimuli (a hug, the right kiss, a certain type of touch, scent, sound), appropriate context (trust, connection, playfulness), and state of mind (feeling calm, confidant, secure), one can become responsively aroused (Basson 2000).

If you're ready to reclaim your sexual desire, the way back is through the body. Learning to safely inhabit your entire being—sensations, feelings, emotions, and thoughts—is the only way to reclaim your sexual power. The exercises in this book are designed to build your capacity to feel safely embodied. Go slow, be patient and compassionate with yourself, and eventually you'll become more comfortable as you reclaim your sexual power.

Sexual Compulsion

For 10 to 20 percent of people, stress actually increases sexual interest, even while blocking sexual pleasure (Nagoski 2015). Some survivors fall into a pattern of reenactment, exposing themselves to situations reminiscent of the original trauma. It's as if they're energetically drawn to repeat the event. This behavior, known as repetition compulsion, repeats in an unconscious attempt to gain understanding and mastery over the traumatic event in hopes of a better outcome. The problem is, mastery is never found. Instead survivors get locked into compulsive sexual behavior that can perpetuate feelings of helplessness, a sense of being bad, or out of control, resulting in further suffering (van der Kolk 1989). There are many ways repetition compulsion can play out. Here are a couple of examples.

Alana met her date for the first time at a bar where he insisted on buying her drink after drink. Between first-date anxiety, conditioning to be agreeable, and pressure from her date, Alana drank too much. Later that evening, he date-raped her. After the assault, rather than avoiding meeting first-time dates alone in a bar, Alana started to date more often, always meeting over several drinks (using alcohol to defend against becoming overwhelmed by implicit traumatic memories) and frequently hooking up at the end of the night. Hooking up would be fine if Alana felt good about it, but in the light of day, she usually regrets her decision. What she really wants is the connection of a healthy relationship, not another one-night stand. Sometimes she doesn't remember consenting to sex and doesn't even like the man. This leaves her feeling further victimized, ashamed, and worthless.

Dylan was raped at age twelve by a grown man in a position of power who pretended to be his friend, all the while manipulating him. Now a young adult, he keeps choosing older men in positions of power to get involved with and is devastated when they eventually betray his trust. This leaves him feeling used, unlovable, and further victimized.

Compulsion happens outside of awareness, it's characterized by dissociation of thoughts, sensations, and emotions related to the traumatic event(s). This numbing, spacing out, or leaving one's body can serve as a protective defense. For some survivors, a sense of self-worth becomes entwined with being desired. Others might see their sexuality as their source of power, yet they keep finding themselves in disempowering situations.

Take a few minutes to reflect. Are you putting yourself in situations that have any similarities to the trau-matic event(s) you experienced?

_____

_____

_____

If so, it may be upsetting to realize this. Your emotions could be ranging of from gut-wrenching pain to regret, shame, anger, or clarity. Acknowledge whatever feelings are coming up, remind your-self repetition compulsion happens outside of awareness, let go of any judgments, be gentle with yourself, and bring in the "Self-Compassion Steps" (chapter 2). Once you become aware of the pattern and begin to process its meaning, the compulsive reenactment is more likely to cease (Bowins 2010). Processing involves working through the procedural, emotional, episodic, and narrative memories (Levine 2015). It's important you also make a conscious choice to not engage in relationships or behaviors that are harmful to you.

Are there any actions you can take to help break this pattern? For example, Alana could refuse to meet first dates in a bar unless she's with trusted friends who agree to look out for her, limit her number of drinks, never leave her drink unattended, or join a support group for addiction if needed.

_____

_____

_____

If you're leaning toward compulsion, revisit the "Dynamic Sexual Consent Assessment Tool" (chapter 6), "Inviting Yourself Back" (chapter 5), and the "Dissociative Experience Log" (online). For further reading on sexuality and trauma, see my reading recommendations at http://newharbinger .com/46509.

— *Story:* It Was All Intertwined

You met Aria in chapter 7. Her story represents how sexual compulsion and sexual aversion can surface as the result of sexual trauma. Aria's grandfather molested her while visiting from abroad from the time she was in kindergarten until she hit puberty. As is common with pedophiles, once she got her period, signaling she was becoming a woman, he stopped. She felt confused and rejected. After all, from a young age, she'd been made to believe that what she later understood to be abuse was the way her grandfather showed his love and adoration for her.

Shortly after her grandfather's rejection, Aria began to seek out self-pleasure; her body was craving it. She would watch porn online, and then feel confused and ashamed of her need for sexual stimulation, not realizing that sexual exploration was a natural part of adolescence. She describes herself as having been "privately hypersexual." The impact of the abuse on her sexuality "was really messy; it was all intertwined."

The sexual compulsion continued into Aria's early twenties. She moved in with her boyfriend of several years, and things suddenly shifted. When they were sexually intimate, she would close her eyes, and the image of her grandfather would appear, creating more confusion. She wondered if this meant she didn't love her partner. Aria became "sexually dormant" and decided to try therapy, "which started dredging things up." She stopped going after three months, and she said, "It helped, but I still wasn't healed. I ran away from it."

Aria married her partner. Several years later, she came to see me. She was still experiencing sexual aversion, resulting in fears of losing her marriage. I explained that many people don't feel spontaneous desire. It's natural not to, especially when suffering from trauma symptoms. We discussed what might help her feel more intimately connected with her husband, and I assigned a body map. Aria identified things that turned her on and some things that shut her down. Then she formulated a few requests for her husband. Meanwhile we continued to work on healing and integrating the trauma.

Several months later, Aria shared, "Now that I'm actually working through it, I'm starting to find my sexuality. I'm more present." She went on to say, "I'm starting to explore other avenues of my sexuality that I didn't know I have." The trauma her grandfather inflicted upon her was no longer intruding on and disrupting her desire, sexual expression, and pleasure.

PRACTICE: Yes, No, and Maybe Body Map

This practice can help bring awareness to your touch and intimacy boundaries. It can be used to inform your partner(s) as to when they need to ask for permission and places that are off limits. It can also be used to track your healing if you've been dissociating or experiencing numbness. You'll need a piece of paper and three colored pencils, crayons, markers, or paint and a brush.

- Draw an outline to represent your body. It can be as simple as the shape of a ginger-human cookie or as detailed and accurate as you want it to be.

- Choose three colors to work with: one to represent yes, one for no, and one for maybe.

- Think of how it feels to be touched, by another with your consent or your own touch, on each part of your body. Color in your map with the corresponding color for where you feel a yes, a no, and a maybe.

- If applicable, does your partner(s) know where your no's and maybe's are? If not, how might you clearly state your boundaries?

_____

_____

_____

- Revisit your map as you continue to reclaim your body. Notice any changes, such as realizing what you thought was a yes is actually a no, or a maybe having become a yes.

Sexual Trauma and Issues with the Pelvic Floor

Sexual trauma can cause the vital organs and energy systems in the pelvis and abdominal organs to go into a kind of shock. These violations often cause a loss of vitality and diminished capacity for erotic connection and pleasure with symptoms such as pain during intercourse. For this reason, some survivors will benefit from seeing a pelvic floor specialist.

The pelvic floor includes the web of muscle fibers and associated connective tissue that span and support the contents of the pelvis, providing support for the bladder, intestines, and in female-assigned bodies, the uterus. When someone is startled by a traumatic event, the pelvic floor, along with the abdominal wall and diaphragm, will naturally tighten. With unresolved trauma, a pattern of constriction may remain.

Pelvic-floor specialists offer hands-on physical therapy that helps rebalance the muscles and structure of the pelvic floor and release stuck or blocked energies. Sessions vary, and at times may involve internal myofascial and energetic-release work. Treatment has the added benefit of supporting a deeper connection with feminine and creative energies. Pelvic floor specialists are trained to explain what they're doing and to ask for consent before any internal work, and you always have the right to say no. Look for a pelvic floor specialist and, if you're female-bodied, an OBGYN who practices trauma-informed care.

PRACTICE: **Pelvic Breath**

This is a simple practice for helping to thaw constriction or numbing in the pelvic floor, one that you can do most any time (without touch). Another benefit is that a relaxed pelvic floor supports grounding. It's okay if you don't notice much at first. With time, you'll feel more. If you notice too much to contain, simply direct the breath to your belly, hands, or feet, and do "Coming into Safety" (chapter 1) if needed.

- Find a safe and quiet place to make yourself comfortable. Go inward and focus on your breath.

- On the inhalation, visualize your breath moving down into your pelvis. You can choose a specific area, or you can send the breath to the entire pelvic floor.

- You can add visualization by imagining that you're breathing in red or orange light, the colors of the root and sacral chakras. As you inhale vibrant glowing light accompanied by your nourishing breath, you energize and illuminate this sacred region of your being.

- Adding gentle touch can support the breath.

- After a few minutes of relaxed breathing, notice what thoughts and sensations are present. Is there movement or a shift in energy? Is desire beginning to be awakened?

There's no right or wrong and no timeline to meet. Simply honor what arises for you. Visit http://newharbinger.com/46509 for another pelvic floor exercise, "Pelvic Motion."

Trauma, Inflammation, and the Vagus Nerve

Health issues resulting from unresolved trauma are another source of grief. Learning the role of the vagus nerve in association with chronic inflammation can help with healing. As discussed in chapters 1 and 2, the vagus nerve is part of the parasympathetic nervous system, which plays an essential role in calming the fight-flight-freeze response and is vital in keeping your body healthy. Made of thousands of predominantly sensory fibers, the vagus nerve reports what's happening in your organs to your brain. The strength of your vagus response is referred to as vagal tone. The stronger your vagal tone, the quicker your body will relax after stress. You may have low vagal tone if it takes you a while to get back to a calm state.

The strength of your vagal tone is measured by heart rate variability, which is regulated by the vagus nerve. When you inhale, your heart beats faster to speed the flow of oxygenated blood throughout your body. When you exhale, your heart rate slows. The vagus nerve is suppressed when you inhale and active when you exhale. When breathing in and out, the bigger the difference in heart rate, the higher your vagal tone. Harmonious or coherent heart rhythms with greater heart rate variability are indicators of cardiovascular health and general well-being.

Low vagal tone has been linked to chronic inflammation, which lies at the root of many, if not most, diseases. The vagus nerve is responsible for switching off the production of proteins that fuel inflammation. Low vagal tone results in the production of pro-inflammatory substances called cytokines, which lead to an increase in stress hormones and sympathetic nervous system activation and can result in systemic inflammation. Given this, it's not uncommon for sexual assault survivors to develop autoimmune diseases and intestinal issues, such as IBS, IBD, and SIBO.

Intestinal difficulties are often related to stress or deeper layers of fear, guilt, and grief, feelings intensified as the result of trauma and co-occurring low vagal tone. As we "swallow and assimilate" reality, if unable to find release, to let go, feelings get locked in the belly. At times we might experience a rush of energy moving upward, a sinking feeling, a feeling of emptiness, or the unpleasant sensation of being punched in the gut (Shapiro 2006).

Are you struggling with any physical sensations or ailments that may be related to inflammation and low vagal tone?

_____

_____

If so, the exercises that follow can help, but first a little more on the heart.

Your Heart, Emotions, and Entrainment

Your heart rhythms mirror your emotional states, and when you feel grief, your heart rhythms reflect this. Emotions usually regarded as negative (fear, anger, disdain) result in disordered and irregular heart rate variability (HRV), while those regarded as positive (love, compassion, gratitude) create improved HRV. Positive emotions also downregulate the sympathetic nervous system calming the fight-flight-freeze response and increase parasympathetic ventral vagal activity (rest and digest, feed and breed). In addition, intuition becomes more accessible when your heart and brain are in coherence.

The body's most powerful electromagnetic field radiates from the heart. The heart's rhythm has the capacity to bring all of the body's systems into a state of synchronization and "entrainment"— where the rhythm of the heart causes other bodily systems to gradually fall into the same rhythm. When the rhythms of the heart become coherent, its electromagnetic field also improves coherence, transmitting waves of healing throughout the body mind and brain. Improved HRV and coherence equates improved health.

Ideally, you're looking for a brain-heart entrainment. To create entrainment, you have to get out of your head and drop into and connect from your heart center. You might feel a little more vulnerable connecting from your heart, but vulnerability is the prerequisite for both courage and creativity (Bowen 2014).

PRACTICE: Heart-Centered Breathing

This practice can improve vagal tone, heart coherence, and entrainment.

- Make yourself comfortable, with your shoulders in a relaxed and open position. Bring focus to your breath.

- Breathe into the center of your chest, the center of your being, as you direct the breath to your heart.

- Begin to breathe a little more slowly than usual, inhaling and exhaling at an even pace of five to six seconds each.

- Give yourself permission to release any tension or stress with each out-breath, seeing if you can settle into a sense of calm and relaxation in your body.

- With each inhalation, imagine that your breath embodies love, warmth, and kindness as you feel your heart begin to soften and open. Inhale love and nurturance; exhale tension and stress.

- To enhance the practice, place one or both hands on your sternum, softly resting across your heart. Notice what sensations are present and the quality of the movement beneath your hands.

- Continue to focus on breathing into your heart center. If your mind wanders, come back to the breath for just a little longer. It can help to think of a positive memory, one that brings about feelings of gratitude, compassion, peace, or love, or to visualize your inhalation filling your heart with light.

- When you feel ready to end the practice, scan your body. Do you feel more open, expansive, calm, or relaxed than when you began?

In addition to the above benefits, taking just ten deep breaths every hour can significantly reduce stress. For a high-tech approach, HeartMath sells a clip-on device to monitor HRV and increase coherence. It offers a detailed look at time and frequency and is used with the Inner Balance app. Apple Watch's Breathe session measures HRV with less detailed information than HeartMath. BreathingZone is an inexpensive app that helps improve coherence without measuring it.

PRACTICE: Abdominal Massage

This practice helps stimulate the vagus nerve, strengthens vagal tone, and supports the reduction of inflammation. Try each prompt for as long as comfortable.

- In a safe comfortable space, lying down, place one hand horizontally on your abdomen under your sternum. Push in and move your hand downward, followed by the other hand, repeating as you get a rhythmic motion going. It's similar to pedaling a bike.

- Place one hand on each side of your torso just below your ribs. Massage downward and inward until you reach your hips.

- Place your fingers just above your belly button and press inward. Moving clockwise (toward your left) make a series of small spirals continuing around your belly button.

- Starting at your belly button and again moving clockwise, make a large spiral around your naval continuing outward until you reach your ribs and hips. Then still moving in a clockwise direction, reverse the spiral as you move inward and back to your belly button.

Having read these last sections on sexuality, and overall health, you may feel a lot of emotion coming up, perhaps more grief for the ways you've been impacted by the traumatic event(s). The "Letting Go Ritual" available at http://newharbinger.com/46509 can help facilitate release of painful feelings after you've taken the time to acknowledge, allow, and accept them.

CHAPTER 9

Your Empowered Self

Your relationship with others begins with your relationship with yourself. How can another know you with any depth if you don't deeply know yourself? Do you have a clear sense of yourself and of how others see you? What drives your behavior, actions, and decisions? Do you know what your strengths are and what triggers your defenses, those times when you react without conscious intention in an attempt to reduce discomfort? When you're empowered, you have self-agency. In order to have self-agency it's helpful to be aware of your character strengths, how you define integrity, and your very essence—which you'll explore in this chapter. You'll learn how to strengthen resilience, what physically supports empowerment, what forgiveness can look like, and how to enhance your vision of your future.

Character Strengths

Self-knowledge helps cultivate respect and compassion for yourself and others. For a greater awareness of your character strengths, I recommend Dr. Martin E. P. Seligman's Values in Action Survey of Character Strengths at http://www.authentichappiness.sas.upenn.edu. There's no charge, but you'll need to sign in to access it and get your results. It's listed as "VIA" under the "Questionnaires" tab and takes about twenty minutes to complete. It will rank your strengths. When you get your results, be sure to look beyond your top five and print out or take a screen shot of your results. Another way to learn your character strengths is to choose a few people you're close to and ask them what strengths they see in you. You can ask that they rate them in order of strength. Be sure to write down what they say.

What are your top five strengths?

_____

_____

_____

_____

_____

Are you surprised by any of your top strengths?

_____

_____

_____

Do you tend to take these strengths for granted?

_____

_____

_____

Are there any strengths in the mid to lower range that you would like to strengthen?

_____

_____

_____

Can you think of some actions you might take to strengthen these traits?

_____

_____

_____

Many people tend to downplay their strengths. They can seem effortless, so they're overlooked. What you might be taking for granted, others are working hard to cultivate. Take a few moments now to appreciate your strengths. They've developed from your unique life circumstances and the choices you've made along the way.

PRACTICE: How Do You Define Integrity?

Integrity is a key character strength. It motivates and inspires you to live authentically as the best version of yourself. To live authentically, you must know your core values and beliefs. What gives meaning to your life, and what is authentically you? Consider what's most important to you and how you contribute in relation to the following applicable areas.

Family:

_____

_____

_____

Intimate relationship(s), partnership(s), or marriage:

_____

_____

_____

Friendships:

_____

_____

_____

Parenting:

_____

_____

_____

Work, career, education:

_____

_____

_____

Creativity:

_____

_____

_____

Play, relaxation:

_____

_____

_____

Physical health, well-being:

_____

_____

_____

Community, society:

_____

_____

_____

Nature, the environment:

_____

_____

_____

Spirituality:

_____

_____

_____

Consider what makes you authentic? How do you authentically show up?

_____

_____

_____

This list represents how you define integrity. To live with integrity, your actions and words must reflect your values. If you find yourself being inauthentic, examine your underlying feelings and motivations. Often anxiety or fear is the underlying cause. Confront any rigidly held beliefs and opinions to be sure they align with your definition of integrity.

Are there any areas you would like to improve upon, and if so, how might you?

_____

_____

_____

_____

_____

Integrity by nature is ever present, whether your surrounded by others or completely alone. The more you align your words and actions with your values, the clearer you'll express your truth to the world, and the more powerful you'll be in manifesting that truth as reality.

Resilience

You are resilient. It is your resilience that's helping you heal. Resilience is the capacity to recover from difficulties and challenges, such as trauma. Adaptive problem solving, emotional stability, mental agility, and adaptability are all indicators of strong resilience. Noam Shpancer (2020) explains that an aspect of resilience is "the ability to assess stressors accurately, face them intentionally, and act on them with courage and purpose" (50). It can be helpful to know that your default mode under adversity is resilience.

The trauma you went through understandably caused you to be more fearful. In *Hardwiring Happiness*, Rick Hanson, PhD, (2013) explains, "Unfortunately, the formation of implicit memory is *negatively* biased…We usually learn faster from pain than from pleasure. Strong dislikes are acquired faster than strong likes" (26). Because of this bias, you'll want to choose to do things that strengthen the internalization of positive experiences in implicit memory (chapter 4). These are the sorts of actions that help strengthen resilience.

"Tapping in the Good" (a play on Hanson's Taking in the Good), mindfulness, the "Egg Boundary," and the "Self-Compassion Steps" are just a few of the many exercises in this book that help strengthen resilience. It can be hard to see how these practices are making a difference until you look back at where you were six months or a year after starting. You met Renee in chapter 6, who regularly draws on the "Egg Boundary" and the "Self-Compassion Steps." After eight months of practice and much progress in her healing, she shared, "Through self-compassion, I can have the *resilience* to face the stuff that triggers me. It's actually stronger than self-deprecation."

Take some time now to reflect on where you were when you started this workbook in comparison to where you are now. How much time has passed, and can you recognize any improvement in your symptoms?

_____

_____

_____

If so, which practices have helped you most? If not, which practices might you incorporate into your daily routine to strengthen your resilience?

_____

_____

_____

Here are some other things you can do to strengthen your resilience:

- Be flexible; accept and face challenges from conscious choice that align with your values and goals.

- Take action and focus on what you can control.

- Broaden your perspective. Think of how someone you admire would respond and imagine what the other person's point of view might be or how you might view the situation in five or ten years.

- Look for at least one positive thing to appreciate as you're going about your day. This trains your brain to look for more.

- Start a daily gratitude practice, for example write down three things your grateful for when you wake up or before bed.

- Nurture your relationships with friends, family, and community.

- Do the "Letting Go Ritual," which you can find at http://newharbinger.com/46509.

- Last but not least, practice self-care.

The practice below is a nice form of self-care that can help strengthen resilience.

Your Essential Self

The word "essence" can be viewed as one's soul, our innate defining substance, as interchangeable with consciousness, the subjective experience of being aware, the sense of knowing and that which is known. So, who are you essentially?

Essence is palpable in babies; as they breathe full, healthy belly breaths, their uninhibited, spontaneous openness to the moment is visible. We all started out this way, but as you gradually learned to communicate with language, you became conditioned to believe you are your personality, and thus began overidentifying with viewpoints and opinions of the ego. As this necessary developmental step took you out of the present into the stories you tell yourself, stories about what should or should not be or have been, your effortless connection with essence was lost.

The mind's stories are necessary. Your identity is derived from your history and the narrative your mind tells you over and over again about that history. You need to make meaning to survive and thrive. The challenge is that the narrative your mind reiterates is limiting. It is only one perspective of many possibilities, often an interpretation that unwittingly creates more suffering.

Much of the unhappiness you experience is not due to the conditions of the moment; rather the mind's evaluation of the moment, what should or should not be, is what causes this unhappiness or suffering. Using the example of frustration many people experience while waiting in long lines at the airport, Eckhart Tolle suggested we ask, "What is it that causes me to be irritated, angry, upset? What is it? Is it this situation, or is it my mind telling me this should not be happening? The ego is very good at misinterpreting reality, and it believes its stories…it's a source of great suffering" (OWN 2017). Observe your thoughts, knowing that you have the choice to change your focus or perspective and not believe or act on every thought you have, instead of letting your thoughts control you.

Mark Nepo (2011) writes, "the essence of our life is the intangible presence at the center of our soul" (117). While difficult to define, you can make contact with your essence allowing that central presence, that pure internal quality, to inform you.

PRACTICE: Meeting Your Essential Self

This exercise can put you in touch with the qualities of your essential self. Connecting with your essential self will help support self-agency and empowerment. It's adapted from Jett Psaris and Marlena Lyons's (2000) beautifully written book, *Undefended Love*. All quotations are by Psaris and Lyons.

Make yourself as comfortable as possible. Scan your body and notice if any tension is present. If so, try giving the tension permission to soften. Then ask yourself if anything's needed. Directing breath to the area, soothing touch, movement, a pillow for support? Once you feel relaxed and present, move onto step number one.

1. Think of a happy memory, one of the most positive moments you've experienced. Take your time. If you have several, narrow it down to the one that stands out most in this moment. If you're struggling to find a memory, know that it doesn't need to be a perfect one, just a short period of time when you felt overwhelmed with positive emotion.

2. Recall the details of the experience and allow the memory to fill your awareness. Revisit and reexperience the qualities from the past and allow them to permeate your consciousness.

3. Write down your memory, describing it "as if you were trying to get someone else to understand and feel exactly what you felt at that time" (37). Engage all of your senses. What details can you remember for each?

   _____

   _____

   _____

   _____

   _____

4. Become absorbed in the memory, bringing the experience into present as much as you're able to. What do you feel and what sensations are present as you recount this memory?

   _____

   _____

   _____

   _____

5. Think of how you viewed others and the world at the time. Was it different than usual in any way? What thoughts, emotions, and sensations stood out in relation to others and the world?

   _____

   _____

   _____

   _____

6.   How was your experience of yourself different from usual?

_____

_____

_____

_____

7.   Underline the positive qualities you listed in steps 5 and 6.

8.   Take a moment to connect with these qualities again as these are the qualities of your essential self. "They are always there—you need only learn how to be receptive to them." (37)

Psaris and Lyons (2000) explain, "When we stop our compulsive activity—in the form of obsessive thinking, worrying, doing, eating, etc.—we increase our ability to experience qualities of our essential self... As we interrupt our usual patterns, our perceptions become increasingly heightened, and we know ourselves as present, open, loving, expanded beings... As we relate in this open, undefended way, we realize that this clear, perfect, pristine, and unwounded core of our being, our essential self, is ever-present. The task for each of us is to listen to and sustain our experience of it" (38).

When you drop beneath the surface of defenses, trauma, and shame, if ever so briefly, you find this clear, perfect, and unwounded core of your being. Simply recall your positive life experience, sensing, feeling, visualizing, and connecting with it deeply as your essence permeates every cell in your body. With time, you can grow your capacity to drop in and sustain your connection to essence, where you are present, nonreactive, spontaneous, and luminous.

PRACTICE: **An Empowered Walk**

Strength and empowerment emerge from a calm, centered, and relaxed body rather than a constricted and rigid one. This exercise is adapted from the work of Paul Linden, PhD, (2004) a specialist in body and movement awareness education, with extensive experience supporting survivors. Paul teaches that a relaxed state "is the foundation for effective and successful action of any sort, and in particular, for effective self-protection" (8–9).

·   Begin by standing and walking around the space you're in. Take note of how your belly feels. Are you tensing or sucking in your gut? If so notice, without judgment, how this affects your breathing.

·   As you continue walking, tighten your belly and pelvic region, gripping your core muscles. How does this affect your movement? Pay close attention to how your legs, hips, lower back, and your breathing are impacted.

- Next, stand in place and alternate between tightening your abdomen and then relaxing it. Your relaxed abdomen should feel familiar from the belly breaths you've been practicing (chapter 1).

- Now release the tightening and stay with the belly breaths. You can place one or both hands on your abdomen and visualize sending the breath to your abdomen as it gently extends out on your inhalation.

- As you continue to breathe this way, consciously allow your pelvic area to also relax. How does it feel to let your abdomen and pelvic floor relax?

- Walk around once again with your abdomen and pelvic region relaxed as you breathe from your belly.

- Now relax your entire body (shoulders, neck, jaw, forehead, hands) along with your abdomen and pelvic region. Notice how this feels compared to your initial walk. Do you experience greater ease, fluidity, and grounding?

This is how walking should feel. You may be so used to walking around with a tense and constricted abdomen and pelvic floor that walking this way feels unnatural or even a little uncomfortable. If you practice this breath exercise often enough, it will become second nature. Your body will begin to shift into it naturally when your nervous system and energy body need to increase relaxation or decrease the fight-or-flight response. You are much stronger and more resilient when you're relaxed and aware than when you're tense and unaware. Relaxation is the foundation for empowerment. Being mindful of your breath also brings you into the present moment, where you can make the choice to not be swept along, instead becoming witness and co-creator of your life.

Trauma has a lasting impact. It will always be part of your past, yet it doesn't have to define you. You can emerge stronger. Try the "An Empowered Narrative" practice, available at http://newharbinger.com/46509.

To Forgive or Not to Forgive

Forgiveness should never be forced. Only you can know if and when you're ready to forgive. In my opinion, forgiveness isn't necessary to heal from sexual assault and can impede recovery if you rush to forgiveness before processing your feelings and beliefs about the assault(s). That said, the act of forgiveness is not about the other person. You forgive for yourself. To forgive others does not mean reconciliation, nor does it mean to condone. It's about releasing resentment toward those who've harmed you. It's about letting go of any hold they have on you, your mind, body, heart, and soul. When you forgive, you give up the hope that it could have been any different, and you give yourself permission to embrace life fully, in this way forgiveness is empowering.

Loving-kindness meditation (LKM), also known as *metta* meditation, dates back to fifteenth-century Buddhism and refers to a mental state of unselfish and unconditional kindness to all beings. The meaning of "metta" is benevolence. This meditation's been used for centuries to develop love and transform anger into compassion. LKM involves gently repeating certain phrases in order to direct positive energy toward other people, as well as oneself.

When you release anger, feel your grief underneath the anger, let it move through, and then forgive (yourself or others), it provides instant balance to certain aspects of the energy body and a feeling of expansion (Chiasson 2013). This level of forgiveness is an art and requires practice. It's okay if you're not now or ever ready to forgive those who've done you harm. You can still benefit from LKM as you honor your connection with whomever you choose and most importantly, with yourself.

PRACTICE: Metta Meditation, Loving-Kindness

Before you begin this version of the LKM, choose someone to bring to mind for the third stanza. Start with someone whom you're experiencing only a small degree of difficulty. After you've practiced enough to feel familiar with LKM, you can choose people and situations where forgiveness is more challenging. As you practice, it's important to bring full awareness to the phrases, their meaning, and any feelings they bring up. Repeat the four stanzas below four or more times each.

May I be at peace.

May my heart remain open.

May I awaken to the light of my own true nature.

May I be healed.

May I be a source of healing for all beings.

(Now Bring into your awareness someone you love.)

May you be at peace.

May your heart remain open.

May you awaken to the light of your own true nature.

May you be healed.

May you be a source of healing for all beings.

(Now bring into your awareness someone you're having difficulty with.)

May you be at peace.

May your heart remain open.

May you awaken to the light of your own true nature.

May you be healed.

May you be a source of healing for all beings.

(Bring into your awareness a group, a system, or all living things.)

May we be at peace.

May our hearts remain open.

May we awaken to the light of our own true nature.

May we be healed.

May we be a source of healing for all beings.

After completing the meditation notice, without judgment, what sensations you feel in your body. Do you feel more expanded or constricted after this practice, and how do you recognize this?

_____

_____

Have your thoughts shifted from prior to doing the loving-kindness meditation?

_____

_____

This is a nice practice to use as part of your daily twelve minutes of mindfulness (chapter 2) and can be combined with toe tapping (chapter 1) or done anytime you're waiting in silence (a long line, on public transportation, in a doctor's office).

PRACTICE: **Empowered Future**

You've been gifted the wonderful ability to create, to envision something that doesn't yet exist, and to work toward manifesting it. To be a cocreator in your life, you must begin with forming a clear view of what you'd like to grow for yourself, otherwise you're swept along without an oar to help you to your destination, the manifestation of your dreams, or the fulfillment of your purpose. This exercise helps align your visions with the results you desire.

- Standing, ground, center, and come into the present moment. Think of something you would like to manifest. If there are several things, choose one to work with.

- Ask yourself: Are there any limiting thoughts standing in the way? If so, what is the negative belief? Turn it around to an affirmation in support of what you're working toward. Find a positive phrase that has meaning and power for you. For example, the limiting thought might be, *I have nothing of value to say,* which might lead to the sentences, *My voice is of value. I am free to express myself.*

- Repeat your affirmation a few times, tweaking it if necessary until it resonates for you.

- Create a visual representation of the phrase you chose. To connect to a visual representation, close your eyes and imagine that the phrase you came up with is part of your beliefs and experiences now. What would that look like? If comfortable, repeat it out loud several times. Does an image spontaneously arrive? If not, envision what you would like to see when you say the phrase. For example, the image might be one of standing outside on a sunny day surrounded by a circle of friends who are attentively and enthusiastically listening to you tell a story.

- As your image takes form, is it accompanied with positive emotions and sensations? See if you can feel the phrase. Where do you feel most alive and in sync with the image?

- Go to this place of aliveness and find a movement to accompany your affirmation and image. This could be a gesture with your hands and arms or a bigger movement with your legs or whole body engaged. In the example, the movement might be one of standing firmly on the ground, legs aligned with your hips, hands over your sternum and heart, and speaking the words "My voice is of value." Then, with your arms moving open, palms facing out, "I am free to express myself."

Repeat this movement, visualization, and affirmation at least two minutes a day for thirty days (or longer). To integrate a new belief, you must feel and embody what you're trying to grow for yourself. Feeling into what you want to create intensifies your ability to manifest your goals. In fact, the clearer you can get with your imagination, engaging as many senses as possible, the better. Affirming brings focus to your internal dialogue, directing it to what you envision and away from worries and fears. Embodying your goals helps take them from vision to manifestation. The future is the potential that lives in you.

In Closing

I'm grateful we've taken this journey together. Thank you for allowing me to walk with you on your path toward healing and empowerment. I hope you'll revisit this book with fresh eyes. As you move forward, new meaning will emerge. For ongoing support, maintain the daily practices of grounding and mindfulness. Bring in the "Self-Compassion Steps," "Coming into Safety," and any of the practices that generate movement toward ventral vagal calm when your nervous system is activated. For help with this, you can refer to the chart "Which Tools to Use When" available at http://www .newharbinger.com/46509. My wish for you is that you continue to ground in your physical body, listening to its wisdom, feeling safe and empowered in your skin, as you reclaim the home that is your birthright.

I invite you to take pause, place your hands on your heart or give yourself a hug, take a deep yet gentle breath, and acknowledge all of the courage, discipline, and vulnerability that was required of you to complete this book. I'm proud of you.

Thanks

I give thanks, recognition, and appreciation to all those who have helped to make this book possible: to the survivors who kindly allowed me to share a part of their story; to my mother, Margaret, for her sacrifice and perseverance; to Beth S., Michaela G., Kysha J., and Miranda Y. for their friendship, encouragement, and support; to Caroline V. for the nudge; to Susanne B. for her generous guidance; to Maria L. and Kysha J. who posed for the illustrations; to Tony A. and Henry R. for their contributions to my education; to the many teachers, therapists, and healers I've learned from along the way, with a special shout out to the late Bill Bowen for his kindness and brilliance, and Don H. Johnson for his vision and manifestation in creating the Somatic Psychotherapy department at CIIS; to the authors quoted throughout the book and those who generously gave permission to include their work; and to the editors and staff at New Harbinger, including but not limited to Jess O'Brian, Jennifer Holder, and Gretel Hakanson. My heartfelt gratitude to each of you.

References

Basson, R. 2000. "The Female Sexual Response: A Different Model." *Journal of Sex & Marital Therapy* 26(1): 51–65.

Black, M. C., K. C. Basile, M. J. Breiding, S. G. Smith, M. L. Walters, M. T., Merrick, J. Chen, and M. R. Stevens. 2011. "The National Intimate Partner and Sexual Violence Survey (NISVS): 2010 Summary Report." Atlanta, GA: National Center for Injury Prevention and Control, Centers for Disease Control and Prevention.

Bowen, B. 2012. Psych-Physical Therapy: Professional Training in Somatic Resourcing, self-published training manual, out of print.

Bowen, B. 2013. Personal communication, October 5.

Bowen, B. 2014. Psych-Physical Therapy: Professional Training in Somatic Psychotherapy, self-published training manual, out of print.

Bowins, B. 2010. "Repetitive Maladaptive Behavior: Beyond Repetition Compulsion." *The American Journal of Psychoanalysis* 70: 282–298.

Brach, T. 2020. Author's personal notes from Compassion webinar, online (January).

Brown, R. P., and P. L. Gerbarg. 2012. *The Healing Power of the Breath.* Boston: Shambhala Publications, Inc.

Caldwell, C. 2018. *Bodyfulness: Somatic Practices for Presence, Empowerment, and Waking Up in This Life.* Boulder, CO: Shambhala Publications, Inc.

Chiasson, A. M. 2013. *Energy Healing: The Essentials of Self-Care.* Boulder, CO: Sounds True, Inc.

Dana, D. 2018. *The Polyvagal Theory in Therapy: Engaging the Rhythm of Regulation.* New York: W. W. Norton & Company, Inc.

David, S. 2016. *Emotional Agility: Get Unstuck, Embrace Change, and Thrive in Work and* Life. New York: Penguin Random House.

Duran, E. 2014. *Healing the Soul Wound: Trauma-Informed Counseling for Indigenous Communities.* New York: Teachers College Press.

Eden, D., 2012. *The Little Book of Energy Medicine: The Essential Guide to Balancing Your Body's Energies.* New York: Penguin Group Inc.

Fisher, J. 2014. "The Treatment of Structural Dissociation in Chronically Traumatized Patients." In *Trauma Treatment in Practice: Complex Trauma and Dissociation,* edited by T. Anstorp and K. Benum. Oslo: Universitetsforlaget.

Gawain, S. 2000. *Developing Intuition: Practical Guidance for Daily Life.* Novato, CA: New World Library.

Haines, S. 1999. *Healing Sex: A Mind-Body Approach to Healing Sexual Trauma*. San Francisco: Cleis Press Inc. Ebook.

Hanson, R. 2013. *Hardwiring Happiness: The New Brain Science of Contentment, Calm, and Confidence*. New York: Harmony Books.

Heiss, R. 2019. From Frozen to Free. *Psychology Today* 52(3): 42–43.

Hicks, J. 2019. "The Intersection of Unconscious Trauma Responses and Sexual Praxes." *The Therapist* 31(4): 18–24.

Juhan, D. 2003. *Job's Body: A Handbook for Bodywork*. Barrytown, NY: Station Hill Press, Inc.

Levine, P. A. 1997. *Waking the Tiger: Healing Trauma*. Berkeley, CA: North Atlantic Books.

Levine, P. A. 2008. *Healing Trauma*. Boulder, CO: Sounds True, Inc.

Levine, P. A. 2015. *Trauma and Memory: Brain and Body in Search for the Living Past, A Practical Guide for Understanding and Working with Traumatic Memory*. Berkeley, CA: North Atlantic Books

Levine, P. A., and M. Phillips. 2012. *Freedom from Pain: Discover Your Body's Power to Overcome Physical Pain*. Boulder, CO: Sounds True, Inc.

Linden, P. 2004. *Winning is Healing—Basics: An Introduction to Body Awareness and Empowerment for Abuse Survivors*. Columbus, OH: CCMS Publications

Miller, C. 2019. *Know My Name*. Penguin Random House, LLC.

Nagoski, E. 2015. *Come as You Are: The Surprising New Science That Will Transform Your Sex Life*. New York: Simon & Schuster, Inc.

Neff, K. 2020. Author's personal notes from Compassion webinar, online (January 23).

Neff, K., and C. Germer. 2018. *The Mindful Self-Compassion Workbook: A Proven Way to Accept Yourself, Build Inner Strength, And Thrive*. New York: The Guilford Press.

Nepo, M. 2011. *The Book of Awakening: Having the Life You Want by Being Present to the Life You Have*. San Francisco: Conari Press.

Ogden, P., and J. Fisher. 2015. *Sensorimotor Psychotherapy: Interventions for Trauma and Attachment*. New York: W. W. Norton & Company, Inc.

OWN. 2019. "Chanel Miller, Stanford Sexual Assault Survivor, On Revealing Her Identity." September 26. https://www.facebook.com/watch/live/?v=490373211543582&ref=watch_permalink.

OWN. 2017. "Eckhart Tolle's Advice That Oprah Says Eliminated All Stress." October 25. http://www.oprah.com/own-super-soul-sunday/eckhart-tolles-advice-that-oprah-says-eliminated-all-stress.

Porges, S. W. 2011. *The Polyvagal Theory: Neurophysiological Foundations of Emotions, Attachment, Communication, Self-Regulation*. New York: W. W. Norton & Company, Inc.

Porges, S. W. 2017. *The Pocket Guide to The Polyvagal Theory: The Transformative Power of Feeling Safe*. New York: W. W. Norton & Company, Inc.

Porges, S. W., and D. Dana. 2018. *Clinical Applications of The Polyvagal Theory: The Emergence of Polyvagal-Informed Therapies.* New York: W. W. Norton & Company, Inc.

Psaris, J., and M. Lyons, 2000. *Undefended Love.* Oakland, CA: New Harbinger Publications, Inc.

Rellini, A., and C. Meston. 2006. "Psychophysiological Sexual Arousal in Women with a History of Childhood Sexual Abuse." *Journal of Sex and Marital Therapy* 32: 5–22.

Rosenberg, M. B. 2015. *Nonviolent Communication: A Language of Life.* Encinitas, CA: PuddleDancer Press.

Rothschild, B. 2010. *8 Keys to Safe Trauma Recovery: Take-Charge Strategies to Empower Your Healing.* New York: W. W. Norton & Company, Inc.

Schore, A. N. 2012. *The Science of the Art of Psychotherapy.* New York: W. W. Norton & Company, Inc.

Shapiro, D. 2006. *Your Body Speaks Your Mind: Decoding the Emotional, Psychological, and Spiritual Messages That Underlie Illness.* Boulder, CO: Sounds True, Inc.

Shpancer, N. 2020. "Designed for Success: Resilience Is in Human Nature. Persevering Through Adversity Is Not a Bug in Our Software but a Feature of the Hardware." *Psychology Today* 53(5): 45–52, 62.

Siegel, D. J. 2012. *Pocket Guide to Interpersonal Neurobiology.* New York: W. W. Norton & Company, Inc.

Stanley, S. 2016. *Relational and Body-Centered Practices for Healing Trauma: Lifting the Burdens of the Past.* New York: Routledge.

Staudacher, C. 1994. *Time to Grieve: Meditations for Healing.* San Francisco, CA: Harper.

Thomas, S. P., M. Groer, M. Davis, P. Droppleman, J. Mozingo, and M. Pierce. 2000. "Anger and Cancer: An Analysis of the Linkages." *Cancer Nursing* 23(5): 344–349.

van der Kolk, B. A. 1989. "The Compulsion to Repeat the Trauma: Re-enactment, Revictimization, and Masochism." *Psychiatric Clinics of North America* 12(2): 389–411.

Verduyn, P., and Lavrijsen, S. 2015. "Which Emotions Last Longest and Why: The Role of Event Importance and Rumination." *Motivation and Emotion* 39(1): 119–127.

Erika Shershun, MFT, is a licensed psychotherapist and supervisor working in private practice in San Francisco, CA. Specializing in treating survivors of sexual assault and incest—and a survivor herself—she facilitates an ongoing weekly group, Surviving and Thriving: Healing Sexual Trauma. A graduate of the California Institute of Integral Studies clinical psychology MA program with a concentration in somatic psychology, she is a member of the California Association of Marriage and Family Therapists (CAMFT), and the United States Association for Body Psychotherapy (USABP). Erika welcomes and values diversity, including all races, sexualities, genders, body sizes, and abilities. To contact her please visit www.healingsexualtrauma.com, www.erikashershuntherapy.com, or follow her @erikashershun.

ABOUT NEW HARBINGER

Founded by psychologist Matthew McKay and Patrick Fanning, New Harbinger has published books that promote wellness in mind, body, and spirit for more than forty-five years.

Our proven-effective self-help books and pioneering workbooks help readers of all ages and backgrounds make positive lifestyle changes, improve mental health and well-being, and achieve meaningful personal growth. In addition, our spirituality books offer profound guidance for deepening awareness and cultivating healing, self-discovery, and fulfillment.

New Harbinger is proud to be an independent and employee-owned company, publishing books that reflect its core values of integrity, innovation, commitment, sustainability, compassion, and trust. Written by leaders in the field and recommended by therapists worldwide, New Harbinger books are practical, reliable, and provide real tools for real change.

FROM OUR PUBLISHER—

As the publisher at New Harbinger and a clinical psychologist since 1978, I know that emotional problems are best helped with evidence-based therapies. These are the treatments derived from scientific research (randomized controlled trials) that show what works. Whether these treatments are delivered by trained clinicians or found in a self-help book, they are designed to p rovide you with proven strategies to overcome your problem.

Therapies that aren't evidence-based—whether offered by clinicians or in books—are much less likely to help. In fact, therapies that aren't guided by science may not help you at all. That's why this New Harbinger book is based on scientific evidence that the treatment can relieve emotional pain.

This is important: if this book isn't enough, and you need the help of a skilled therapist, use the following resource to find a clinician trained in the evidence-based protocols appropriate for your problem.

Real help is available for the problems you have been struggling with. The skills you can learn from evidence-based therapies will change your life.

Matthew McKay, PhD
Publisher, New Harbinger Publications

If you need a therapist, the following organization can help you find a therapist trained in cognitive behavioral therapy (CBT).

The Association for Behavioral & Cognitive Therapies (ABCT) Find-a-Therapist service offers a list of therapists schooled in CBT techniques. Therapists listed are licensed professionals who have met the membership requirements of ABCT and who have chosen to appear in the directory.
Please visit www.abct.org and click on *Find a Therapist*.

MORE BOOKS from
NEW HARBINGER PUBLICATIONS

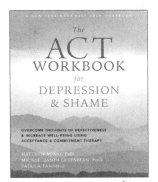

**THE ACT WORKBOOK FOR
DEPRESSION AND SHAME**

Overcome Thoughts of Defectiveness
and Increase Well-Being Using
Acceptance and Commitment Therapy

978-1684035540 / US $22.95

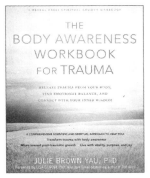

**THE BODY AWARENESS
WORKBOOK FOR TRAUMA**

Release Trauma from Your Body,
Find Emotional Balance, and
Connect with Your Inner Wisdom

978-1684033256 / US $21.95

REVEAL PRESS
An Imprint of New Harbinger Publications

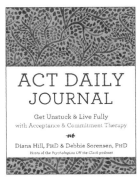

ACT DAILY JOURNAL

Get Unstuck and Live Fully with
Acceptance and Commitment Therapy

978-1684037377 / US $18.95

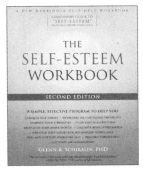

**THE SELF-ESTEEM
WORKBOOK,
SECOND EDITION**

978-1626255937 / US $22.95

SUPER-WOMEN

Superhero Therapy for
Women Battling Anxiety,
Depression, and Trauma

978-1684037520 / US $18.95

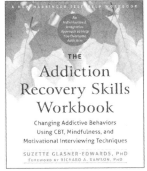

**THE ADDICTION RECOVERY
SKILLS WORKBOOK**

Changing Addictive Behaviors
Using CBT, Mindfulness, and
Motivational Interviewing Techniques

978-1626252783 / US $25.95

Register your **new harbinger** titles for additional benefits!

When you register your **new harbinger** title—purchased in any format, from any source—you get access to benefits like the following:

- Downloadable accessories like printable worksheets and extra content

- Instructional videos and audio files

- Information about updates, corrections, and new editions

Not every title has accessories, but we're adding new material all the time.

Access free accessories in 3 easy steps:

1. Sign in at NewHarbinger.com (or **register** to create an account).

2. Click on **register a book**. Search for your title and click the **register** button when it appears.

3. Click on the **book cover or title** to go to its details page. Click on **accessories** to view and access files.

That's all there is to it!

If you need help, visit:

NewHarbinger.com/accessories

new harbinger
CELEBRATING
40 YEARS